DIARY OF A NORTH AMERICAN RESEARCHER IN BRAZIL III

Mark J. Curran

Order this book online at www.trafford.com
or email orders@trafford.com

Most Trafford titles are also available at major online book retailers.

Print information available on the last page.

ISBN: 978-1-4907-7764-1 (sc)
ISBN: 978-1-4907-7771-9 (e)

Trafford rev. 10/19//2016

www.trafford.com
North America & international
toll-free: 1 888 232 4444 (USA & Canada)
fax: 812 355 4082

Table of Contents

Dedication

Looking again at "Retrato do Brasil em Cordel" by Ateliê Publishing Company in 2011 in São Paulo and seeing the "Thank you" page, one sees the people from the Brazilian academic world who facilitated research in Brazil from the initial year of 1966 through 2002. I consider "Retrato" to be the most serious, most complete and best researched and written books of all my efforts to capture the story of the Brazilian "literatura de cordel."

Now in 2016, completing the series "Stories I Told My Students" in this third volume of anecdotes of trips to Brazil, I would like to use yet another list. The reader will note that Volume I of this series had the title of "Adventures," the second "Chronicle," and now in Volume III "Diary." There is a reason for this choice of words. The purpose of the narration has changed and evolved over the years. In this narrative of the final moments spent in Brazil – research, travels, conferences, book publication and book signings, tourism, socializing, solitude and sadness, happiness and moments of triumph – the tone of the narration is different. This final volume is essentially an account based on trip diaries.

I will of course write of intellectual moments at the conferences, the quirks of such events in Brazil, the talks given, but equally important are the encounters with new friends, poets of "cordel," iconic figures of northeastern culture in Brazil, and perhaps most important encounters with old friends who took care of me in both happy and difficult moments over the years. In sum, it is the continuation of the love affair with Brazil, the Brazilians, the "literatura de cordel," and the support of friends in Brazil and of my wife Keah over the years. To all them I dedicate this book. The list will be chronological with encounters in this volume from 1988 to 2005.

I. Poets of "Cordel" and artists in related fields
Gonçalo Ferreira da Silva
Azulão (João José dos Santos)
Abílio de Jesus
Sinésio Alves
Expedito da Silva
Franklin Machado

Téo Azevedo
J. Barros
Ulysses Higino
J. Borges
Zé Lourenço
Valdeck de Garanhuns
Jerônimo Soares
Gerardo Frota
Vânia Frota
Marcelo Soares
José Costa Leite
Varnesci Nascimento
José Alves Sobrinho

II.   Intellectuals, Researchers and Writers
Adriano da Gama Kury
Homero Senna
Neuma Fechine Borges
Edilene Matos
Ildásio Tavares
Raquel de Queiróz
Ronald Daus
Ariano Suassuna
Liêdo Maranhão
Edison Oliveira
Carlos Cunha
Orígenes Lessa
Ivan Cavalcanti Proença
Myriam Fraga
Sérgio Miceli
Plínio Martins
Assis Ângelo
Jerusa Pires
José Aderaldo Castelo
Audálio Dantas
Joseph Luyten
Rosilene Melo
Ivone Maia
Gutenberg Costa
Arnaldo Saraiva

III.   Friends and Hosts
        Henrique and Cristina Kerti
        Flávio and Alice Veloso
        Mário and Laís Barros
        Edilene Matos
        Carlos Cunha
        Neuma Fechine Borges and José Elias Borges
        Luís Raimundo Fernandes
        Roberto Previdi Froelich
        Michael Grossman
        Audálio and Vanira Dantas
        Zé Rubens and Abigail
        Sízio Araújo
        Joseph and Sônia Luyten

        And to Keah

LIST OF IMAGES FOR THE BOOK "DIARY OF A NORTH AMERICAN RESEARCHER IN BRAZIL III"

1 Copacabana in the fog and pollution
2 Curran in the bookstore with his new book on Rodolfo Coelho Cavalcante and the "Modern Literatura de Cordel"
3 "Caipirinha" in the Othon Hotel, Rio, 1988
4 Henrique and Cristina Kerti in Rio, 1988
5 Mark and the Kertis in Rio, 1988
6 The room in the "Pousada São Francisco:" Brahma beer, J. Borges woodcuts and books on "cordel"
7 Curran in a hammock after the beach, Recife
8 The professors, Recife and the conference
9 Neuma Fechine Borges and others, the conference
10 Official photo of the conference, Recife, 1988
11 Curran with the famous Raquel de Queiróz, Recife, the conference
12 Ariano Suassuna and his art
13 Liêdo Maranhão, folklorist and writer, and the author, Olinda
14 Carlos Cunha and Curran, Salvador, 1988
15 Abílio de Jesus and the typography, Salvador, 1988
16 Mário, Laís Barros and family, Itapuã 1988
17 Mark on the beach at Itapuã
18 The "cordel" poet Gonçalo Ferreira da Silva, Rio, 1989
19 Curran at the library of Orígenes Lessa at his home
20 Henrique, Cristina, Letícia Kerti and friends, Rio, 1989
21 Curran and the Kertis
22 The Kertis at the "Hotel Glória"
23 Time for confession
24 Mark and Henrique Kerti, Hotel Glória, 1989
25 Mark and the portrait of Emperor Dom Pedro II, "Hotel Glória"
26 Mark and friend Luís Raimundo Fernandes, Rio
27 Edilene Matos, Carlos Cunha, Salvador, 1989
28 Barra Beach, Salvador, 1989
29 Manaíra Beach, João Pessoa, 1989
30 The remodeled "Pelourinho," Salvador, 1990
31 Mark, the Exu t-shirt, the "Fundação Casa de Jorge Amado," Salvador
32 Book covers from the Amado exposition and Curran's book on Jorge Amado
33 The "Our Lady of the Rosary" ["Nossa Senhora do Rosário"] church in the "Pelourinho"
34 Bruno, Carlos, Carol and Edilene at home

Preface

As promised years ago, now I begin Volume III of the adventures of the naïve "gringo" researcher in Brazil. This is perhaps the last in the series "Stories I told my students" and aims to bring to the present research, writing, professional life, teaching Brazilian Portuguese and Brazilian Culture, and tourism in Brazil during a career of forty-three years. The book will be the continuation of the love affair, the passion and the vocation during the adult years of my life as a professor of Spanish, Portuguese and Latin American Studies at Arizona State University in Tempe, Arizona. I think it may be worthwhile to recall the theme of the series.

Volume I, "Peripécias de um Pesquisador 'Gringo' no Brasil nos Anos 1960" (the version in English was "Adventures of a 'Gringo' Researcher in Brazil in the 1960s) dealt with my first encounter with Brazil, a period of a little more than a year on a Fulbright-Hays Research Grant to do research for the doctoral dissertation on "popular literature in verse" ("a literatura de cordel") and it relation to erudite Brazilian Literature. A young Curran got to know Brazil for the first time and thus began the love affair with the country and its people. The book told about research and living in Recife, the Northeast interior, in Bahia, in Rio, along the São Francisco River in Minas Gerais and Bahia, and at the end in Belém do Pará and Manaus. Through research hints and counseling by Ariano Suassuna, Luís da Câmara Cascudo, Manuel Cavalcanti Proença, Sebastião Nunes Batista and others and a good collection of the short narrative poems and long "romances" of the "popular literature in verse," I took the first steps toward the Ph.D.

Volume II "Aconteceu no Brasil – Crônicas de um Pesquisador Norte Americano no Brasil II" (English version "It Happened in Brazil – Chronicle of a North American Researcher in Brazil II") continued the various stays in Brazil, Curran now a professor at Arizona State University. The book treated research on "cordel," contact with researchers and writers of erudite Brazilian Literature, time with the poets and publishers of the "literatura de cordel," interesting moments at literature conferences and commemorations in Brazil (including the "Fifty Years of Literature of Jorge Amado" celebration in Salvador da Bahia), the not always pleasant task of publishing my writings in Brazil, trips for literary prizes and finally pleasant tourism with my wife Keah. In this volume the form and spirit was closer to the "crônica brasileira" or Brazilian short non-fiction chronicle.

Now in Volume III I will bring to the present the times in Brazil. This phase marks the end of the lengthy research trips to Brazil. The stays now will be shorter due to various reasons, although still involving the collection of "cordel." Volume III will be much more along the line of a travel diary. The book is flavored with vignettes of people, places, and happenings in the "odyssey." It will emphasize participation in conferences in Brazil, the reading of academic papers, and more importantly, spending time with the poets, professors and writers of Brazilian Literature, Northeastern Literature and "popular literature in Verse." So I will describe the conference in Recife in 1988, another in João Pessoa in 1989, and the Brazilian Studies Association Conference in Recife in 2000 (with a pleasant reunion with mentor Ariano Suassuna). A happy moment is the autograph party for my book "Cuíca de Santo Amaro – Poeta Repórter da Bahia" at the Jorge Amado Foundation in Salvador in 1990. Another is the unforgettable meeting of Átila de Almeida in Campina Grande where we talked and I was able to peruse probably the best private collection of "cordel" in all Brazil.

Something different in this final phase of research, writing and professional life will be the time spent in the city of São Paulo (a new setting in my professional career). A special moment will be participation in a unique event" "100 Years of 'Cordel'" sponsored by the SESC-POMPEIA in São Paulo in 2001 where I was able to meet important "cordel" poets I had not met before and renew the friendship with others from past encounters. In addition I met Joseph Luyten after years of correspondence and even more – I met and spent a lot of time with Audálio Dantas, a good friend and one of my favorite Brazilians.

And there was the task of publishing important works in my professional career, including time with Sérgio Miceli, President of the University of São Paulo Press and the publication of "História do Brasil em Cordel." In addition I met Plínio Martins who would publish my "career" book at Ateliê Publishing House in São Paulo, "Retrato do Brasil em Cordel." There would be new friendships in São Paulo and unforgettable tourism on a memorable trip to Iguaçu Falls.

Additional moments in São Paulo would be the friendship with Michael Grossman my guide to the "northeastern world" of São Paulo and time with Téo Azevedo at "Rádio Atual' and the atmosphere of the northeastern cultural centers in the city. To top it off I met the true icon of Northeastern Culture in São Paulo, Assis Ângelo. And I should not forget the friendship with Abigail and Zé Rubens who hosted me in the "Paulista" metropolis in 2002.

The final professional conference was in João Pessoa in 2005 with a nifty "northeastern fair" with "cordel" featured; this was when I met some important personages of "cordel" for the first time: José Costa Leite, José Alves Sobrinho and the young master Marcelo Soares. There were new researchers, principally the feminine voices of Rosilene Melo and Ivone Maia. And finally this was my last meeting with Neuma Fechine Borges, research colleague going back thirty years.

Sandwiched in between all the above will be beautiful personal moments, great reunions with former ASU student Roberto Previdi Froelich in Rio and new encounters with old friends Henrique and Cristina Kerti, Carlos Cunha, Edilene Matos, Mário and Laís Barros in Salvador, and Flávio and Alice Veloso in Recife. There are many travel notes of these encounters, stories from their families and photos as well. They "saved my life" socially over the years (I almost always traveled alone in Brazil.) And I cannot forget them and others of Volumes I and II. The reader will note my moments of solitude and sadness on certain trips, the times when I was not with the friends already mentioned.

Being a bit of a "romantic" in those final years of experiencing Brazil, I did more than one "goodbye tour" to my beloved Brazil, remembering happy, sad and sometimes difficult moments. I shall tell it all. And like Volume I and II when appropriate I will comment on the economic, political and social times.

Perhaps an unnecessary point of curiosity: the reader will note my repeated remarks on the service and food on the flights to Brazil (in this volume from 1988 to 2005 but as well in the total series from 1966 to 2005). These normally introduce the successive chapters. For the jet setter they will be pretty unimportant stuff, but for me, the occasional traveler, and certainly for any reader who has not had similar opportunities, they may be of interest. One will note the evolution of "tourist class" travel over four decades. I have already written that due to very simple tastes in food (perhaps a result of growing up on a wheat farm in Kansas, and perhaps of a very fragile stomach which I have the bad fortune to possess), I never investigated nor could afford "fine cuisine" or gourmet food in all those years in Brazil. My loss! It is an important dimension of Brazil absent in my books.

And the reader will see as well in the three volumes of travels in Brazil that I frequently comment on the price of meals, in "cruzeiros, cruzeiros novos, cruzados, reais" and dollars. Pardon me, but save just one or two occasions in forty-three years, I had a very modest travel budget, particularly taking into account I was a "gringo" in Brazil. It's a minor thing, but it belongs in the narrative.

I never dreamed in those final moments of 2005 that I would return to Brazil years later, but now in different clothing – that of the staff of Lindblad -National Geographic Expeditions on the National Geographic Explorer Ship, this in 2013, 2014, and once again in 2016. On such occasions with a totally new purpose and perspective, I would get to know parts of Brazil never dreamed of, examples being Fernando de Noronha and other scenes south of Rio de Janeiro to the border of Uruguay.

Possibly, I hope, there will be more trips and moments to tell. "Se Deus quiser" (God willing), the love affair of almost fifty years with Brazil and the Brazilians has not arrived at its end.

Chapter I

THE TRIP TO BRAZIL, 1988. INVITED TO THE "CONFERENCE ON NORTHEASTERN LITERATURE" IN RECIFE

Motive: The conference had as its purpose to remember the famous "Conference on Northeast Regionalism" by the master Gilberto Freyre in 1926.

The flight

There were no problems from Phoenix to Los Angeles, then a wait of twenty-five minutes for the luggage, then the "free" shuttle to the new international terminal, the latter filled with Asians from China, Korea, Japan and other nations. I spent the time reviewing old academic articles I had written (to be sharp for the conference in Recife) and enjoyed the sandwiches packed by wife Keah for the trip. Varig was very efficient with the flight leaving on time, a direct flight from Los Angeles to Rio de Janeiro, 11 hours of flight time. We were traveling on a 747 and I was on the upper deck. I found myself seated to the side of a travel agent of "metaphysical vacations." For some reason, our conversation was brief.

The inflight service was that of Varig of the times, better than that of the U.S. carriers, but not up to the level of my former flights in past years with Varig (Was this treatment an imitation of the U.S. flights or just the inevitable change in the times?). The meal was a bit mysterious to me, perhaps planned for the passengers from Tokyo; there was a sort of Asian green beans, beef and rice with a different flavor, cold cuts and dessert. There was a scotch from Varig which helped to pass the time. I think I managed to sleep only thirty minutes in the entire flight, snoozing a little and arriving exhausted in Rio. I forgot: I had the worst breakfast of my life on Varig – a sort of sausage and very strange eggs.

Arrival at the Galeão International Airport and first days in Rio

Visibility was lousy upon our arrival, terrible pollution mixed with fog. I exchanged some dollars at the Varig counter, made the reservation for Recife and then went outside and caught the "frescão" or airport bus to the Hotel Novo Mundo in Flamengo. My room faced the bay with a good view but with terrible noise. Thinking to myself, "Hey, it's only a couple of days, I can take it." The tariff was $34 USD on the parallel market.

Copacabana in the fog and pollution

As always, it was depressing to see the North Zone of Rio arriving to the "Ilha do Governador," where Galeão International Airport was located, the filth and such. Upon arriving in the South Zone all improved including my mental attitude. I was overwhelmed, as always, by the traffic and the noise. Exhausted, I forced myself to make the necessary phone calls, finally succeeding in talking to my first Brazilian friend, a colleague of studies at Rockhurst College in Kansas City, Missouri, at the beginning of the 1960s, Henrique Kerti, who now works in Novo Friburgo, his business to do with frozen storage for meats.

I then caught a bus to the Fundação Casa de Rui Barbosa where I had a conversation with good friend Adriano da Gama Kury. His wife Wilma is in France, daughter Lorelai has just gotten married, and son Adriano Jr. is now a specialist in biology. The father is rightfully proud – his son has just discovered a new spider species (arachnoid) and has an article in a scientific research journal in the U.S. Adriano seems older; he was in Cataluña in 1986 and also in Germany.

Adriano reports that it is very difficult for Brazilians to pay the federal income tax these days, the government watching such things more closely. He spoke of research colleagues from my past days at the Casa: Marco Antônio Nedu is back at the Casa; Maria Eduarda Lessa is in the Literature Section; and there is no news of Sérgio Pachá. There are no less than two hundred copies of my book on Rodolfo Coelho Cavalcante gathering dust in the storage area of the basement of the Casa, this because there is no advertising or marketing budget for distribution of the book (all this was forewarned by Carlos Cunha in Bahia years before). The book was a co-production of the Casa and the very prestigious Nova Fronteira Publishing Company. Too bad.

Other news: the famous French researcher on the "cordel," Raymund Cantel of the Sorbonne has passed on; his widow has inherited his vast collection of "cordel." An aside: Sebastião Nunes Batista's collection is now as well in the library of the Casa (it should be a fine one).

Adriano said that Marly of Lençois Paulista (the reader of Volume II may recall that she was my host and guide in 1985 when Keah and I made the trip to the interior of the State of São Paulo and to the small city of Lençois Paulista to receive a very modest literary prize for "Grande Sertão: Veredas e a Literatura de Cordel"). Marly has left the directorship of the library in Lençois and wants nothing to do with it or the prize or the promised publication of my study. Homero suggests I speak with Ivan Cavalcanti Proença at José Olympio Publishing House regarding the matter. I can't handle that right now. I will write him a letter someday.

Rio de Janeiro, a good day

I slept like a log that night waking up at 8:00 a.m., this in spite of the infernal noise emanating from the front of the hotel. The dining room, however, is on a higher floor in the rear of the hotel facing a quiet park (in fact it is the famous park-garden of the "Palácio do Catete" [The Catete Palace] where President Getúlio Vargas committed suicide in 1954). The breakfast that morning was calm and good: slices of pineapple, watermelon, wonderful French bread, cheese, and tasty "café com leite." The clients of the hotel seemed to me to be middle class, almost all Brazilians, many from the business world. As mentioned, the large breakfast salon has a direct view of the Catete Palace Park with all the tropical plants and trees, a very pretty scene.

I caught a bus that made its way slowly (what a change) to Ipanema and I walked along the sidewalk by the beach perhaps as far as the "Hotel César Parque" before turning around. I then walked along Visconde de Pirajá to do some shopping but was sidetracked by the showcase of H. Sterns Jewelry store advertising "folk art." I'm a sucker for that anytime so went in to this very high end store for wealthy Brazilians and foreign tourists to have a "look around." They did have a few items from the Northeast, but the employees seemed to not have the minimum idea of what they were selling.

Curran in the bookstore with his new book "A Presença de Rodolfo Coelho Cavalcante na Moderna Literatura de Cordel"

I then went to several bookstores in Ipanema – the "Diz Dão", the "Sicicilano" and I finally found copies of my book on Rodolfo Coelho Cavalcante (the same one gathering dust in the basement of the Casa de Rui Barbosa). I confess to being a bit proud. I was then quite happy to find the recent books by Luís Fernando Veríssimo, an author I had utilized for many years in classes at A.S.U. and who inspired the format of Volume II of this series.

The mid-day meal was a large filet with vegetables. Looking outside, it was either very foggy or highly polluted, I can't say for sure. But the temperature was great, perhaps 26 degrees Centigrade with a nice breeze from the ocean.

"Caipirinha" in the Othon Hotel, Rio, 1988

For old times' sake I went to the 30th floor of the Othon and then to the third floor lounge with its broad view of Copacabana beach to have a drink, a "caipirinha" (see the photo). The best thing was the memories of earlier times – Keah and I there in 1985. One new thing: I heard some men speaking a strange language, one I had never heard before. It was Guarani; they were Paraguayan musicians entertaining in the hotel. Our conversation was in Spanish. They were dressed in regional folkloric dress of Paraguay, a bit similar to that of the natives of Guatemala I was much more familiar with; it was a new experience.

There was some shopping, finally finding a nice present for daughter Katie. I owed her one: on this trip I was using her small film camera carried in my briefcase, I was nervous to be carrying a camera in the open in view of those thieves in Rio!

I caught a bus to the Hotel Novo Mundo and from my room saw the Bay of Guanabara at sunset, high sea freighters, fishing boats, and the shuttle flights at Santos Dumont Airport (Rio-São Paulo-Rio), recalling those beautiful scenes from the original "Black Orpheus" in the late 1950s. There were the ubiquitous soccer games along Flamengo Beach and its park and the "aterro" or freeway from Botafogo to downtown. I counted sixteen lanes of traffic between the beach and the hotel! So, although modest lodgings, the view from my room was worth it.

I took a shower and waited on a return phone call (recall these are the days prior to cell phones) from Henrique Kerti. While waiting I made some very naïve notes on my impressions of social class and race in Rio, saw some TV including the old national news program, "O Repórter Esso" or maybe "O Repórter Globo," and a program highlighted in those times – Xuxa and the kids.

Rio de Janeiro, an encounter with the Kertis

Henrique and Cristina Kerti in Rio, 1988

Mark and the Kertis in Rio, 1988

I was picked up by the Kertis at the hotel and we went to their house for dinner. Tomorrow the 16th is Henrique's birthday, his 45th (I am 47). Christina is his wife; their daughter Letícia is twelve years old and a cutie pie. They live on the big avenue facing the "Lagoa Rodrigo Freitas" and you can see the Christ statue from the apartment window.

Henrique's mother Penha, my hostess in those times of 1966 and 1967, is still alive; she lives near the Copacabana Palace Hotel on "Avenida Nossa Senhora da Copacabana;" she lives with Cristiano, Henrique's brother, married in 1968 and divorced in 1978. Henrique and Cristina were married in 1970.

Cristina studied Letters, suffered from throat cancer two years ago, but is doing well now. Henrique has had two open heart surgeries in São Paulo. We have gotten along really well. He is not of an intellectual bent; he likes movies, TV, reads little, but spends long hours at his job, this in Nova Iguaçu, "a meat packing business."

The family firm, "Lojas Americanas," was the victim of a stock takeover involving 35 per cent of the shares; as a result Henrique lost his post in the company, that is, his job, but he is applying the profit from the sale of the shares of "Lojas Americanas" in investments. He says that the family was very well remunerated for its share in the company. He added that he does not need to work, but he does out of pride and for the family. I believe it.

A humorous aside: He and Cristina made a "Marriage Encounter Weekend" at a Jesuit Retreat House, something she calls "brain washing" ["lavagem cerebral"]. (The reader may recall my wife Keah and I were active in this "Movement" in Arizona in the 1970s.) In order to participate in the Encounter, one had to have studied in a Jesuit prep school or university. Henrique is furious with the new "Progressive Jesuits," the Theology of Liberation, and the social changes resulting from it. He is currently searching for a good high school for their only daughter Letícia, but now doubts the local high school of the Jesuits, Saint Ignatius. He wants Letícia to know English and computer science. He does seem to me to be a bit naïve as to computers (remember the date). He has good memories of our university days in Kansas City, Missouri, at Rockhurst, of my mentor in Spanish Vernon Long, and school buddies like Bryan Butler and Eduardo Matheu of Guatemala.

Like many other Brazilians, the Kerti family went to Orlando and Disney World and Epcott Center in 1984, and he tells of being robbed on that occasion. He lost travelers' checks in dollars and their passports "worth ten to fifteen thousand dollars on the black market." It all happened in a shopping center in Orlando. I'm speaking of this, and it is ironical, because of writing so many times over the years of the atmosphere of fear of robbery or a mugging in Brazil and my efforts to avoid such a thing. Even with all this, Henrique said that it was an "incredibly enjoyable trip!" I do not know if I could have maintained the same attitude had such a thing happened to me in Brazil.

Henrique is very pro-USA and very anti-communist; he says he almost moved the family out of Rio to Lisbon, this using the profits from the sale of the family investments, but now it is no longer possible.

We had a very pleasant night together with before dinner drinks, beer, and a dinner of beef, carrots and rice. They dropped me off at my hotel at three o'clock in the morning! I slept only about four hours, having to get up to pack my bags, take a shower, etc.

The Kertis really enjoyed the photos that I had brought along from our life in Colorado. They have a small country "farm" outside of Petrópolis, but rarely go there. They say it just gives them headaches, so they pretty much ignore it.

Another day, the checkout in Rio and the flight to Recife

After a very slow check out at the Novo Mundo I took a taxi well ahead of time in order to arrive without a hassle at the Galeão. The flight to Recife was full and included a Brazilian soccer team on board. There were lots of clouds and rain that morning in Rio. They say that "winter" arrived late this year.

Recife

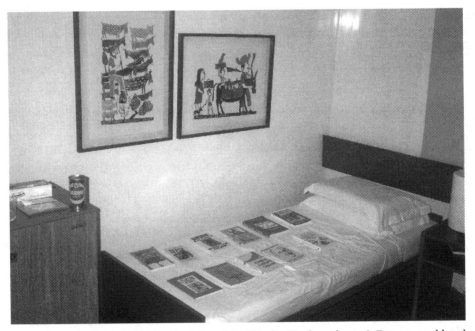

The room at the "Pousada São Francisco" in Olinda: Brahma beer, J. Borges and books

Professor Ormir and Abuendia were waiting for me at the Recife airport and they took me via the outer loop freeway (everything was different now in Pernambuco) to Olinda and the "Pousada São Francisco," a small, modest, yet delightful hotel one block from the beach. I like the atmosphere of the place. The people who gave me the ride know of Tiago and Marcus Amorim (the artists in the "ateliê" in Olinda where I lodged for two weeks during my first trip to Brazil in the 1960s). Tomorrow I will take a walk around Olinda, recalling former places and feeling the nostalgia of it all. It seems quite hot to me and with a lot of humidity, yet, the sea is beautiful! I am very happy to be lodging in Olinda; the Federal University of Pernambuco, the site of the conference, is eighteen kilometers distant from here by city bus. The program seems to be a bit "heavy" to me; we shall see.

Arriving at the hotel I chatted a bit with Ormir, in charge of the conference, an ex-Benedictine priest and now head of the Department of Literature of the UFEPE for the last two years. His specialty is João Guimarães Rosa and the topic of religion in his works. Why did I receive the invitation and why am I here? It was Neuma Fechine Borges (UCLA 1970 conference, coordinator of the Research Library of Folk Popular Poetry of the Federal University of Paraíba) who remembered her friends! I told Ormir that my talk would have to do with Ariano Suassuna; it turns out he is going to be honored at the conference. I met Professor Angela from the University of Salsburg in Austria; she compares the "romanceiros" of Portugal and Brazil; it is her first time in Brazil (speaking of this, I reckon it to be my tenth trip to this country).

An Aside: I ate dinner that first evening in the hotel, having a lengthy conversation with Luís Antônio, a young man from the interior of São Paulo State. He is a black man, thirty-five years old, married with three children, and is here for a training period in management for a clothing factory. We had an unhurried conversation about race in Brazil, his struggles and successes, and the black role models for him from the United States (Martin Luther King), as well as his love for professional basketball in the U.S. and particularly for Magic Johnson. He was born and lived for fifteen years in a small city fifty kilometers from Lençóis Paulista, the tiny town where I received the modest literary prize in 1985! A small world! In his school the ratio of whites to blacks was 99 to 1. He finished high school at night and has been working full-time since he was twenty-two years old; he now has thirteen years with the company. He said, "This is something unheard of in Brazil, me, black, being lodged IN THIS HOTEL!" His plan is to stay in the hotel the balance of this year and then bring his family to Pernambuco. He wanted to have a military career, but being black he would never have been able to rise above the rank of sergeant. He laughed at the notion of "lack of racial prejudice" in Brazil (a concept bandied about my many of its citizens).

Another day, an encounter with Flávio Veloso

I got up at nine and had breakfast with Professor Angela – pineapple, orange juice, cheese, ham, Brazilian pound cake, and delicious "café com leite."

There was a long outing to the beach north of Olinda with an old friend from Recife in the 1960s, Flávio Veloso, and his now wife Alice and their young daughter Mirtes (I "chaperoned" them during the engagement some years back!). We were going to Alice's parents' beach house, Jorge and Mirtes Guimarães, near "Maria Farinha" Beach, and more immediately to Itamaracá Beach. The conversation was good as was the dinner – "casquinha de siri, peixe agulha, cerveja, peixe de coco, lasagna, feijão, arroz, salada de legumes, fruta (sempre abacaxi) e bolo de chocolate." What a feast! Alice's father has a boat and likes to go fishing for "peixe agulha" ["needle fish"] at night.

It is the busiest time of year for Flávio; sugar cane harvest in the Northeast is beginning. He says, "It's crazy." He is contracted by several refineries to trouble shoot the electric machinery. When he works Alice stays at her parents' house in the city. Flávio stays out on the plantations until the problems are solved, at times all night long.

An Aside: The entire hotel in Olinda is decorated with woodcut prints by J. Borges, even in all the guest rooms and the dining room! The reader may remember that the cover of my first book in Brazil was a woodcut representing the miracle of Father Cícero in the mass when the host he gave to the holy woman Maria de Araújo turned to blood in her mouth, thus starting the legend of the "miraculous" priest. The woodcut was done by no less than J. Borges who years later would become famous in all Brazil and in the exterior for his woodcut art.

It was almost impossible that first night to catch all of Flávio's Portuguese (it had been difficult years before as well, probably due to a hearing problem I have, but also the Pernambuco accent). Flávio's father, Dr. Pedro a retired Admiral in the Brazilian Navy and medical doctor is still writing. Sérgio, Flávio's brother is a doctor and has his own practice. Marcelo, the "baby" of the family, is an engineer employed by a French firm in Chile dealing with oil exploration.

Curran in a hammock after the beach, Recife

Some trivia about the family; Alice studies English. Their honeymoon was for one month to Miami, New Orleans and the Bahamas. We did a walk on the beach and "winter" is still very much visible: dirty water, that is, if you do not go out to deep water far from the beach, but the temperature was fine, hot! They insisted that later I come here to their summer house, bring the family, and we would even have the cook for our vacation. Ha ha. It never happened, not their fault.

Upon returning to the hotel I slept badly; there were mosquitoes in the room.

First night of the conference

The professors, Recife and the conference

Neuma Fechine Borges and others, the conference

The first meeting of the group in the hotel was that night – many people from Bahia and Rio and from outside of Brazil – Ronald Daus (Germany and the theme of northeastern banditry), Fred Williams (Santa Barbara, the theme of Maranhão), and Angela (Salsburg, the theme of the European "romanceiro"), and yours truly.

The Bahians are complaining to Ormir about the bad organization of the conference; there is no love lost between the two States, i.e. Pernambuco and Bahia. It was difficult to comprehend the lack of manners on the part of the Bahians.

My friend and host of the days in Salvador, Edilene Matos, is here; her talk will be about Jorge Amado and the "Literatura de Cordel" (there was no problem; it was a quick review, and took nothing away from my previous studies). She gave me a copy of her new book, a work for her Master's Thesis, "O Imaginário no Cordel." It treats four story-poems only and employs critical literary theory. Carlos Cunha is still at the "Academia de Letras da Bahia" and a new affiliate of the Joaquim Nabuco Research Institute in Salvador. Now with her Master's Edilene is lecturing at the Catholic University of Bahia, the Pedro Calmon Foundation and still at the Cultural Foundation of the State of Bahia. With the change in government everything is topsy-turvy. The Cultural Foundation of the State of Bahia now has less funding and prestige. And there is a new foundation – the "Fundação Casa de Jorge Amado" and it does have funding.

The next day at the conference

I° CONGRESSO INTERNACIONAL DE LITERATURA NORDESTINA
Departamento de letras e mestrado em letras e linguística - UFPE
Realizado de 12 a 16 de setembro de 1988 · RECIFE · PE

Official photo of the conference, Recife,1988

We all boarded the bus to the conference and it took a while by the Recife beltway to arrive at University City. The protocol was as follows: the formal "call to order" ["chamada à mesa"], photos for the newspapers, the first speech by Maximiano Campos now the Secretary of Culture and Tourism for the State of Pernambuco, "baroque" in style, with a pleasant homage to the principal invited guest, the famous writer of the "Novelists of the 1930s" ["Romancistas de 30"] Raquel de Queiróz.

I had various conversations with Raquel and she treated me kindly. We talked about Leonardo Mota, "Cego Aderaldo," Luís da Câmara Cascudo ("Cascudinho"), Ariano Suassuna and Graciliano Ramos, really the major figures of Northeast Culture in my era of research during graduate school dissertation research in Brazil. She invited me to visit where she lives in Leblon, in Rio. I've got to get her book "Lampião." Funny, she made me think a little in the sense of personality of my wife Keah's grandmother in Arkansas, but of course, Raquel is a personage in the world of Brazilian Culture, i.e. Literature. She was great throughout the conference, the "star" of it all, a person full of humor and common sense to boot!

On another evening I had supper on the beach with Flávio and Alice. We ate "pitú," a sweet-water shrimp, the name coincidentally that of the most famous sugar cane rum ("cachaça") in Pernambuco and lobster in its own sauce, the two enough alone to be served without sides. The place was extremely noisy so I had great difficulty in understanding Flávio once again. His news: he now has a house on the beach but there was erosion around the foundation so he is understandably very unhappy about that. He work takes him from Alagoas State to Paraíba State. They seem very happy.

The conference, "Thinking to myself"

I liked Angela of Salsburg a lot; she is a quality person. Ronald Daus and his wife admit they are here in Brazil mainly for the tourism (they will go to the "Pantanal" after the conference).The book on northeastern banditry was actually his Ph.D. dissertation, something from a long time ago; he has never returned to the topic. He does administration in Berlin. I liked Neroaldo Pontes de Azevedo very much, a professor of Literature at the Federal University of Paraíba and a specialist on Brazilian Modernism and the "Movement of Northeast Regionalism." He was a serious scholar and person. (Later on in 2005 he will be Secretary of Culture of the State of Paraíba.)

I met a person whose name was familiar to me, Professor Luís Tavares of the Federal University of Ceará; unbelievable! there is actually a Department of "Cordel" at the University, showing now in 1988 how far "cordel" in terms of prestige has come these past years. Luís is now Vice-Rector of the University. He gave me his book on "cordel." Thus it is that I am getting to know people that I have needed to meet for a long time. My priority was however to meet those involved in Pernambuco State, the area where I had done original research in the 1960s.

The second night of the conference, an encounter with Hélio Coelho

I went to the home of an old friend and one of my "guides" in Pernambuco in the 1960s, Hélio Coelho, an old colonial home in Olinda now completely restored (it probably was 400 years old!). As expected it was a veritable art museum with painting, ceramics and Pernambuco folklore. I thought to myself, really, all that I know about northeastern folklore should be shared. But how?

Hélio has a Ph.D. in nuclear physics and his work takes him to the U.S., Canada, Europe and Japan. He travels about eight times a year to the main university in São Paulo; he is Director of Theoretical Nuclear Physics at the University of Pernambuco. Once in a while he goes to see Aldemir, his brother who is a retired physician I happen to know in Arizona. So the house I describe is on one of those hills in Olinda, an old colonial mansion, beautiful, with many Portuguese tiles, a beautiful garden with fruit trees of the Northeast, and a swimming pool. There is a view of Recife, albeit from a distance. Hélio says it is the perfect place to work, mainly quiet, no small achievement in Brazil! He also has a house in Gaibú (Hélio was part of the girls and guys in our social group who did an outing to that beach in 1966). So the reunion was good with great conversation, but Hélio now an adult, seemed quite serious, "all business." In fact he seemed to me to be a bit "fechado" as the Pernambuco folks say, "serious and to himself," and maybe not the carefree youth I remembered.

I did impose on him one item for nostalgia reasons from those old days – a visit to a Xangô religious ceremony. We went to the old "terreiro" or "temple" of Pai Edú, a "father of the saint" of the 1960s and the first place I was introduced to Xangô in Brazil. You can't go home again! Pai Edú now seemed to me to be completely full of himself; he was dressed in red velvet, like a gypsy, for it happened to be the "night of the gypsies" in the ritual. There now was champagne for the dancers, chants done via microphone, and no drumming. An Aside: The intellectual and writer, professor Ildásio Tavares from Salvador, is an "ogan," [male participant,] in the "purest candomblé rite" in that city, this according to him in a later conversation. We only stayed half an hour at the "Xangô," a ritual I enjoyed so much in 1966.

The third day, other moments, an encounter with Raquel de Queiróz and the festive night with the professors from the conference

I stayed in the hotel making reservations for Salvador on Friday, writing these notes and revising my presentation at the conference. I'll catch the bus this afternoon to "Cidade Universitária" for the session. I attend most presentations only with great difficulty, but I have kept totally busy since Sunday.

In the afternoon it was like old times in the 1960s. I went to downtown Recife, catching the bus in Olinda, a "local" or "pinga-pinga" as the northeasterners call it, full of black kids "hitching a ride, "bats" or "morcegos" as the local parlance puts it. It was rain, heat and sweat all the way to town. I had lunch in a local spot near the old Law School, the "Lai-Lai," eating the blue-plate special of Chinese food and conversing with some young ladies. Then I walked across the bridge to the old downtown and eventually to the old Penitentiary – the infamous bandit Antônio Silvino of "cordel" fame was prisoner there (it's worth a look at his story: he reformed his life totally and made enough money while in prison to educate his children!) The building is now a tourist market with small shops in the old prison cells selling clay dolls ["bonecos de barro"], chess sets made of the same clay, leather maps and mainly tourist "gadgets" ["bugigangas"]. I saw a few story-poems of "cordel" but only found five new ones of interest.

Back at the hotel there was talk with Ronald Daus and his companion Angela, incidentally blond with long hair and sexy at that! (Am I revealing my stereotyped knowledge of German women?)

Later I went to the old São José Market in old Recife and visited the "cordel" stand of Edson Pinto, my main source of story-poems all the way back to the 1960s.

The market was jammed with people; this is the "other Brazil." The market itself was being "remodeled," and it was a mess. The entire old tiny Plaza where I witnessed the performance of the poets of "cordel" had a wooden construction fence around it. Not particularly animated about all this, I made my way through that labyrinth of streets and alleyways back to the bus and the hotel.

Curran with the famous Raquel de Queióz, Recife, the conference

There were various conversations with Raquel de Queróz in the hotel, on the bus to the conference (I helped her climb on and off the bus; she is now advanced in age). She was very kind to me ["gentil"], very "simpática." It was great. I need to read her "Dora, Doralina," her story about the São Francisco River and the old wood burning stern wheelers (one of the most folkloric trips in Brazil back in the 1960s, sadly now reduced to one tourist boat).

That night many folks from the conference went to the restaurant "Rei da Agulha" in Olinda and it turned out to be a pretty wild night. There was conversation with Esman of the UFEPE, in charge of the foreign student exchange program; he appeared a little like the hippies of the 1960s. I also talked with Luís Tavares, Vice-Rector and head of the "cordel" program at the Federal University of Ceará. We hit it off well. And I also talked a bit to Antônio Beckman of the Federal University of Maranhão; he is initiating the "cordel" program there.

The main "feature" of the night was an extemporaneous "show" – the Bahians and the Cariocas! There was beer, garlic shrimp, "langostino" – all for 4000 CR, a good value. It was a long night of improvised verse by Ildásio Tavares of Salvador and Pedro Lyra of the Federal University of Rio de Janeiro. I caught just a fraction of it, but gathered it was a mixture of the serious and the ribald, mainly the latter. The group of female professors from UFBA were there – scholars all – Dora, Elizabeth, Maria Conceição, Ívia and Edilene.

When those entertaining improvisers of verse work, they do serious work. Ildásio is unbelievable, a veteran of the old Left from the 1960s and 1970s. He is a poet and is a Full Professor of Portuguese Literature, but knows North American Literature well. He does like to "show off" at these meetings, the improvised poetry vulgar and satiric, modeled on the old "epigrams" of the Bahian oral tradition. As mentioned he improvised poetry with Pedro Lyra well into the wee hours of the morning.

At this juncture I can say I know well the routine of the academic conferences in Brazil, including the entire goings on. The one in Rio back in 1973, told in Volume II, was more international in tone, more in line with Portugal, more serious with less of the university atmosphere of Brazil.

There was time for private conversation with Ildásio. In a few words he basically told of the intellectual life and its quarrels and scandals in Bahia. In sum: the politics is unbelievable and includes even bad feelings bordering on hate, directly for me from the pages of "The Miracle Shop" ["Tenda dos Milagres"] the novel of Jorge Amado.

Fourth day at the conference – an incredible day and Ariano Suassuna

Ariano Suassasuna and his art

The first talk was the history of Theater in Pernambuco from 1945 to 1985 by a very serious professor. It was followed by an amazing "show" of two hours in length – the "return to public activity" by Ariano Suassuna. He is celebrating his first new play in twenty-five years marking the "return to public life and writing." Up to this point he was temporarily out of the classrooms. The response by the audience was near "delirium" ["delírio"] and was compounded by an emotional scene with Ariano and Raquel de Queiróz with many "grandes abraços." At that point Ariano gave a serious talk on the Theater of the Northeast and how he combines the best of European dramatic tradition with the Northeast: "commedia dell'arte" and "cordel."

Suassuna is a master of the anecdote, of telling stories; he spoke of "Nascimento Grande", a popular personage of old Recife during the times of Leandro Gomes de Barros (I have the "cordel" classic in my collection), of the bureaucracy in the University, and of his youth in Taperoá. It was an extraordinary moment, the first time I had actually witnessed the "jeito" by Ariano created in what he called "spectacle – classes" ["aulas – espetáculos"]. These have become famous in Brazil and were recently televised for a national audience. He spoke of the culture of the "sertão" or backlands of the Northeast, of Europe, of the "Movimento Armorial," an artistic movement created by him in the 1970s. An Aside: I had given him a copy of my book "A Presença de Rodolfo Coelho Cavalcante na Moderna Literatura de Cordel", just out in 1987, published by Nova Fronteira in Rio, and the whole time he talked he was waving his hand in the air with the book in it. The audience was on its feet, ["uma louvação em pé"] with shouts, applause and laughter.

The big mistake

Woe is me! Because I had asked for an earlier time for my talk, they placed me directly after Ariano's "show," in a sort of panel discussion (instead of the original format of talk and debate). My take on the whole thing: the talk was too formal. I tried to tell some of my own anecdotes and it did not turn out particularly well. My talk on Jorge Amado was just "okay," nothing of what I am capable of doing. In sum it was not up to par. One can imagine the scene: following the great showman Ariano! No need to say more; it was a lesson in humility for sure.

An encounter with Liêdo Maranhão and the premiere of Ariano Suassuna's new play

Liêdo Maranhão, folklorist and writer, and the author, Recife

Later that day I want to Liêdo Maranhão's house in Olinda. It was a long overdue encounter; I had known of him and read many of his books in the past years. He is a true folklorist and has captured much of Recife lore. He had incredible photos of the "cordel" poets of the 1970s (collectors' items for sure), one particularly ironic in nature: Rodolfo Coelho Cavalcante, Minelvino Francisco Silva, João José da Silva, José Costa Leite, Zé Bernardo da Silva and J. Borges together. One could not have wished more for the "encounter in 'cordel' heaven!" The best thing was that the occasion was a wedding, and all were dressed in tuxedos! - an unheard of scene. All those photos have disappeared as far as I know; where they went who knows!

Liêdo has perhaps half a dozen of the old story-poems of Leandro Gomes de Barros, more than 300 woodcut blocks, and more than twenty years of notes, hand-written, about folklore and "cordel." He asked me for financial help for an idea – "The Museum of the People" ["O Museu do Povo"] to be placed near the São José Market. He has a new book: "Sex in the Words of the People" ["O Sexo nas Palavras fo Povo"]! Liêdo never shied away from such topics! He helps the "cordel" poets and the poet-singers with donations for dentists and doctors and is the only one here doing this. Liêdo seemed a bit full of himself, a little arrogant (perhaps he deserves to be, I think so). He had a falling out with the Joaquim Nabuco Foundation. His entire library is located in a very moldy, humid room at the back of the house. I made no promises, how could I without funding resources even for myself at ole' A.S.U.?

Later that night all the conference attendees went to the premiere of Ariano Suassuna's new play, I was with the Daus's; he commented in passing that he had received an offer from UCLA for $100,000 per annum, but had turned it down. Life for him is based in Germany and he travels the world. Úrsula is his second wife; she directs a literary review in Berlin. He now is a specialist in Third World Literature; he goes often to Japan; they were both very kind to me during dinner that night. We saw the premiere of Ariano's play with his classic use of hidden identity, "armorial" costumes and northeastern music. It was a highly emotional moment with the artist's presence at a full house performance.

Conclusions, Recife, 1988

On the negative side, taking into account some boring talks, the presence of some "prima donnas" of the intellectual world, plus the negative comments of Ildásio Tavares, it was still entertaining. The positive hugely outweighed the negative. The hotel was fine and I succeeded in making and renewing all the possible contacts with my interests of northeastern literature and "cordel." It was good for the ego; I felt appreciated and liked by the Brazilians after the long years of work. One recalls that there were 400 to 500 people in the audience each day and many asking for autographs; it is another world. Imagine such a scene in an academic conference in in the United States! It was a hoot.

The Northeast in Pernambuco still seems provincial, still re-living the era and the fame of Gilberto Freyre. A case in point was Roberto Mota's presentation and homage to his father who was the main administrator of the Joaquim Nabuco Foundation in my days of research in the 1960s. They love homages, debates, and the personal touch; it all provides a good lesson in Brazilian Civilization! Someone at one point in the conference, in an aside, said that he prefers "The tales of the struggle of the poor outlander and the days of the bandit Lampião to the shit and corruption of the present day politicians, "shirt and tie gunmen" ["pistoleiros de colarinhos"]. (The theme of politics and corruption will surface throughout this book and the seventeen years it entails.) The comment was received with wild applause by the huge audience. An Aside: Seeing the debacle of recent years, the new heights of greed, bribery, political gifts and outright corruption of 2016 and the imminent impeachment of Dilma, and the widespread dishonesty of those who want to impeach her, 1988 was tame indeed!

An Aside: Ronald Daus thinks that basically neither the Northeast nor the Brazilians have really changed much since the 1960s. I agree but only up to a certain point.

Departure from Recife, the stop in Bahia after the conference

In the Guararapes Airport of Recife I noticed a short, elderly priest walking to the gate; not totally certain I asked, "Sir, are you Dom Helder Câmara?" He quipped, "No. I'm his brother." Indeed it was ***the*** Dom Hêlder. Years earlier my wife Keah and I had first seen him, we in the highest rows of the huge auditorium of the Eucharistic Congress in Philadelphia in 1976, he receiving together with Mother Teresa the homage of all present. He will be remembered as the "Red Bishop" of the National Council of Brazilian Bishops, as living in the era of Liberation Theology, and especially for his famous statement: "The greatest violence is hunger." The reader may recall my comments on him in the first of this trilogy – "Adventures of a 'Gringo' Researcher in Brazil in the 1960s."

I purchased a bottle of "Pitu" that we nursed for years in Tempe. The plane to Recife was the milk run ["avião pinga-pinga"], and then I took the "frescão" bus along the long sea shore to the Hotel Bahia do Sol in Salvador.

First day in Salvador, an encounter with Carlos Cunha and Edilene Matos

It all started with a phone conversation with old friend and guide for Bahian folklore Carlos Cunha. He reported that he had placed many notes in the local papers about my book of 1987 about Rodolfo Coelho Cavalcante; one might recall that on the occasion I did not go to Brazil nor was there any autograph party, probably due to the modus operandi at the time of the Rui Barbosa Foundation, its co-editor. Cunha again counseled me (always in his own interest) to publish my book on Cuíca de Santo Amaro in Salvador. It was the usual "silver-tongued" Carlos. I did make a decision at the time to leave the manuscript at the Cultural Foundation of the State of Bahia where both he and Edilene Matos worked.

That night was one of those; I ate supper alone at "La Pergola" near the hotel: "bife, fritas, tomate, cebola" and an icy beer to wash it down. The cost: $4.50 USD.

The next morning there was a good breakfast in the hotel including good pineapple. I took the Barra Bus to the Barra Port and the Mauá Institute for shopping; it was here that I discovered the enameled, painted tiles ["azulejos"] of the Bahianas that decorate our kitchen in Mesa today. The Institute was not open when I arrived so the time was spent with one of my favorite pastimes – observing "life" in Barra. Some black kids ["moleques"] were playing handball and badminton on the beach; others with small handcarts were bringing stuff to the beach – nets, chairs, etc. to rent to tourists. Many folks were exercising on the beach and yours truly noticed a lot of "dental floss" ["fio dental"] swimsuits on Barra Beach. To top off the scene there was clear water, just medium waves and a few small fishing boats moored off shore.

Poverty however was very much evident at the same scene: "street children" ["pivetes"] sleeping on top of the bus stop made in the form of a concrete "U," waking up and peeing right there. And there were many beggars; all seemed in a state of abandonment. So my conclusion was: the beach and sea beautiful, the rest extreme poverty.

Carlos Cunha and Curran Salvador, 1988

I met Carlos Cunha at the Cultural Foundation of the State of Bahia and shortly thereafter he took me on one of his customary "fast walks" through the city: the Elevator Lacerda to the lower city and the "Praça Cairu." The "Mercado Modelo" seems the same as a few years ago; Camaféu de Oxossi (a minor character in several of Jorge Amado's novels) sold the restaurant on the third floor facing the bay but it looks the same. One recalls that this was my hangout or "ponto" in research days from the 1960s, the 1970s and up to the present date.

Cunha in a long conversation brought me up to date on folklore and "cordel" in Bahia: Rodolfo Coelho Cavalcante was run over in heavy traffic in his home "bairro" of Liberdade and was rushed to a hospital with horrible conditions, no equipment, definitely a "poor man's hospital." There was no blood supply so they had to try to find some, somewhere, somehow, nearby. Rodolfo died after an attempted surgery to fix his wounds. The Cultural Foundation paid for a "first class funeral" ["um enterro de primeiro"]. There were many notes and notices in the newspapers, eulogies on Television, a TV special on Rodolfo, and Jorge Calmon (Salvador's main newspaper and media person) and other dignitaries appeared at the funeral. Cunha had, by the way, predicted all this as early as 1981 when I researched my book on Rodolfo; notwithstanding the career of "cordel" poet and publisher, Rodolfo was a "personage" in Bahia. This is one of the cultural aspects of the city that outsiders need to understand: popular figures like Cuíca de Santo Amaro, Camaféu de Oxossi, Capoeira "Mestre Bimba, artist of "cordel" covers Sinésio Alves, and various "mães de santo" are just a few cases in point.

Now in 1988 Cunha reports that "cordel" in Salvador is moribund with little "movement." The "Núcleo for the Study of the 'Literatura de Cordel'" in the State Cultural Foundation still exists, but there is very little activity. Edilene keeps busy with various projects on Jorge Amado and "cordel" in Bahia.

The newspaper journalist Paulo Marconi never did finish his promised book on Cuíca de Santo Amaro. Cunha said that now, in these days, there is very little interest on the muckraking "cordel" poet. In the case of my manuscript and book about Cuíca, the printing cost to do such a book is high; if I do not pay it will not come out. Cunha at that point spoke with great candor: all the writers in Salvador pay the publishing cost of their own books; there is no "stigma" to this simply because there is no other avenue to publish. Everyone understands this, so the large part of the writers follow the practice, a sort of Vanity Press.

Abílio de Jesus at the typography, Salvador, 1988

Later there was an encounter with a master of the old style typography – Abílio de Jesus. He works for Cunha and together they print books for the Joaquim Nabuco Foundation's branch in Salvador. We have written about him and his life previously. Cunha has something on his mind, "a flea in the ear" ["uma pulga na orelha"] as they used to say in Brazil. He says my study on João Guimarães Rosa and the "literatura de cordel" would be great for the Jorge Amado Foundation in the "Pelourinho;" the director Mryiam Fraga (I met her first in 1980 at Jorge Amado's "50 years of Literature" commemoration) according to Cunha is a "serious person ["boa, profissional"]. And besides, João Guimarães Rosa has never been published in Salvador. He says if it does not come out at José Olympio Publishing in Rio (the manuscript is presently pigeonholed there), send it on up to Bahia. I said, "I'll think about it."

Carlos then proceeded to give me an update on "cordel." Retired General Umberto Peregrino has a new book on "cordel" in Rio, and there is also another by Veríssimo de Melo in Rio Grande do Norte State, but there is little interest in popular culture or folklore. Guimarães Rosa is another matter!

Cunha talked of the book "industry" in Salvador: there is no major publishing house, thus all the "free-lancing" of vanity publishing discussed earlier - print locally with a small press. The most prestigious among them at present is that of the Federal University of Bahia, but the author pays all!

All the above conversation took place in the restaurant of the Market with a beautiful sea in the background. There was personal news about Carlos and Edilene. They are remodeling the house; Carlos is working at the local branch of the Joaquim Nabuco Foundation, at the Cultural Foundation of the State of Bahia and as executive director of the Academy of Letters of Bahia ["Academia de Letras da Bahia"]. He is limited in earnings because he does not have a university degree. Edilene with a university degree earns considerably more, but with a strenuous work load.

Reunion with the Barros in Itapuã

Mário, Laís Barros and family, Itapuã, 1988

Mark on the beach at Itapuã

We had a great visit; they enjoyed seeing the photos of Keah and Katie. Mários's parents are very "simpáticos;" Carla now is thirteen years old and looks like Laís, and Eduardo is eleven. They just finished a vacation to Disney-Epcott in Orlando; curiously enough it was cheaper than traveling to southern Brazil where they are from, this in 1986!

Mário complains about the bad economic times in Brazil (what else is new?), saying the company is struggling to stay in business. Just the same life in Bahia is not all that bad; the beach is as beautiful as ever, but there are thieves about on the nearby beach near the Hotel Quatro Rodas. Mário's English is EXCELLENT! He travels a lot to São Paulo and to Porto Alegre; the holding company for his firm has its offices in Porto Alegre. With the firm Mário is representing several Japanese and American firms in the area of heavy agricultural equipment and equipment for road construction. There are 150 employees in Salvador and 60 to 70 in the interior of the State of Bahia. Mário is in charge of the State of Sergipe and Bahia, heading the financial department. He says he spends 70 per cent of his work day applying the company funds in investments, this just to protect the capital with Brazil's raging inflation. He is pessimistic about Brazil's future (what can he be thinking now in 2016?), but says it is too late now to make any changes. He wants the kids to do high school in the U.S. either via American Field Service or a similar exchange program. He thinks the kids can choose either Canada or the U.S., but he repeats that things are bad in Brazil at the moment. I noticed the barbed wire and bits of broken glass embedded on the top of the outside walls of his house; there has been a history of break ins in the neighborhood.

An unexpected moment at the airport in Salvador and the flight to Rio de Janeiro

At 6:30 a.m. my flight was first delayed and then cancelled. I switched carriers to Transbrasil, the plane arrived, but the crew had excess flight time so must rest. So the passengers waited until almost midnight for a fresh crew to arrive from Rio. Although it was almost midnight when we departed for Rio it was still a relief just to be on our way.

Resting at the Othon Hotel in Rio due to the "arrangement" by Varig Airlines

In Rio it was in fact chilly with rain and clouds but you could see the cargo ships coming through the outer limits of the Bay of Guanabara. I return to the "adventure" of the flight from Salvador: it turns out there were problems with the landing gear in João Pessoa, and the aforementioned problems with the crew in Salvador. Better late than dead! However, Varig Airlines was great; upon our landing and arrival at 3:00 a.m. the Galeão Airport was empty. The staff however was waiting for all of us, so I made a reservation for the Miami flight that evening. They provided us with a voucher for the "radio taxi" to the Hotel Othon, including the tariff for one night, all meals and a three-minute international phone call home. Recalling the atmosphere prior to arriving in Rio, that of the airport at Salvador from 8 p.m. to midnight - the passengers were angry and there was much confusion. It was a new experience but now I was confident all would go well to Miami.

Even at the Othon I slept badly (too exhausted to sleep if that makes sense), and awakening from fitful sleep went down to the breakfast buffet at 9:00 a.m. There was an interesting conversation with some Chilean businessmen here for a seminar in Teresópolis. They defended the military regime in Chile (Augusto Pinochet) and the recent payment to the IMF. They cannot believe the economic "confusion" in Brazil. Thinking to myself: "With the current political, economic and social situation in Brazil maybe I'll change jobs and just become a "library researcher" in the USA. A little joke.

Still in the hotel, killing time, I looked at the Olympics on TV as well as Brazilian basketball and a volleyball match between the U.S. and Brazil. This was the first and only time I had watched television on this trip. Still thinking to myself: "I've got to eat again shortly, go to that great bar on the third floor which overlooks the beach and have a last "caipirinha," and take a nap before the next part of the travel "Odyssey."

The international phone call was easy (I am not accustomed to this at all): dial 0 for the hotel, then 001, then the number in Arizona, direct dialing to home in Mesa. It was good to hear Keah and Katie's voices; I would be very soon.

The hotel was full of foreigners, most speaking Spanish. I actually preferred the modest "Pousada" in Olinda, that is, with the exception of the third floor bar at the Othon. I enjoyed a bountiful buffet early afternoon: "fatias de maminha de alcatre, arroz e feijão, tomates, e vinho para regar" ["to wash it all down"] – this plus the view of Copacabana Beach, the sea gulls and the ocean. It was a grey, windy, rainy day but the hotel was full. The price in 1988 was interesting: 57.000 cruzeiros for the room, 62,700 with the ten per cent tax, or $125 USD. The main luncheon buffet was 3.500 CR or $8 USD.

I did the checkout at 7:00 p.m., Varig taking care of the bill, This was followed by the Radio Taxi to the Galeão (the driver's wife is employed by a North American); it was raining hard along the way.

At the Galeão I talked to Luciana (the Varig employee who had arranged everything for me that preceding night at 3:00 a.m.) and I offered to write a letter of recommendation for her work is she so desired. Later I was in line with my bags, she came up and said, "Wait here." Twenty minutes later I found myself in Executive Class (the only time ever before or since in Brazil). I wrote the letter. Then I described the trip in English:

Varig Executive Service (only time ever)

Slippers, tote bag with toiletries, magazines, newspapers and hot towels

Drinks including champagne and peanuts

Cold plate: two jumbo shrimp, golden caviar, olives

Hot plate: delicious "bacalhau," beef filet, rice served buffet style

Dessert: fruit, three kinds of European cheese, two pastries, "cafezinho" and Drambuie

All on fine china with pattern, gleaming silverware and "Varig" crystal

A bit better than tourist class! I imagine this service has changed just a bit from 1988 to 2016.

Although I was lonely and lost one day of travel time, the consequences were interesting: the Othon and Executive Class on Varig. The flight was eight hours to Miami and one experienced the shock of the clean monorail trip from the international to the national terminal, passing through customs quickly and without having to open my bags. (Try that in 2016!) So it was "on board" Eastern Airlines to Los Angeles, a flight of four hours, fifty – three minutes and then the short flight to Phoenix. All in all it was a success.

Conclusions, Brazil 1988

There was a terrible financial crisis, people living in the streets, the middle class near to drowning in a sea of misery, losing ground each day (it made me think of an equivalent situation in the United States in 2009). The mania for politics continued: an atmosphere of corruption and of fear and worries if Brazil were to survive. "I will not hesitate to speak of all this to the students at ASU or whitewash it either; they have to know the truth. The problems of Brazil may be too large or complex to solve. People in the street say that the masses cannot organize and there are no means for revolution. There are many Brazilians who believe the country is heading directly into chaos and the Apocalypse! It makes me fear for our own future in the United States, writing now from 2009 after the latest Stock Market collapse. It is clear that the United States has lost international prestige; true economic power seems to have passed to Japan, Western Europe in this era of great change. I thought to myself: our faith and perseverance will be tested in the future! Am I wrong? I hope so."

When I compare the contrast of the last ten days in Brazil with our life in the United States it is difficult to believe. It is going to take a few days for me to return to the "routine" life at home in the U.S., to rest and "maintain the line." An Aside: the US dollar is now the base of the Brazilian economy; the market for dollars and for gold is what greases the wheels.

This marks the end of travel notes from 1988.

CHAPTER II

TRAVEL TO BRAZIL IN 1989

Motive – I was invited to João Pessoa by research colleague Neuma Fechine Borges to participate in a seminar on "popular literature in verse" at the Federal University of Paraíba.

The flight and the first moments in Rio

There was a sad goodbye to Keah and Katie in Phoenix, then a long waiting line for the Varig check in in Los Angeles, in fact one hour and forty minutes wait. The flight was thirteen hours with a stop in Panama with good conversation with the Varig people on the way.

The inflight service on Varig was excellent at least in comparison to TWA or other American airlines. First came the piping hot towel to "refresh oneself," then the menu in three languages, a movie, music, cocktails, and a tasty meal of filet mignon. After the three hour flight to Panama and takeoff there was another meal like the first. After nine hours into the flight after Panamá came breakfast; the "gringo" required only an orange juice. Compare this flight with that from Tokyo a few years earlier.

There was a small fright due to waiting an hour and one half for my luggage to arrive; it had come on another flight from Los Angeles. I had thought of this possibility while still in Los Angeles with all the international traffic and apparent confusion.

I caught the big bus, "o frescão," to the Hotel Novo Mundo in Flamengo (recall I was on a very modest budget). The city was calm due to being Sunday morning but there was a lot of election material in view along the way. The room was fine with a view of the beach, ocean and Sugar Loaf off to the right, but there was tremendous noise. I took a quick shower and in spite of being exhausted from the travel, caught a city bus to the Northeastern Fair in São Cristóvão (because it was Sunday and this would be my only opportunity to "hit" the market on this trip). My impressions: it was depressing, dirty and with much poverty in evidence, but still quite large with the food and beer stands and the roaring sound from the "forró" music stands.

Encounter with the "cordel" poet Gonçalo Ferreira da Silva at the São Cristóvão Fair

The "cordel" poet Gonçalo Ferreira da Silva, Rio, 1989

I saw Expedito da Silva's poetry stand, his son the woodcut artist Everaldo da Silva, and then Gonçalo's stand. He had just started the "Brazilian Academy of the 'Literatura de Cordel'" ["Academia Brasileira da Literatura de Cordel"], modeled I think on Rodolfo Coelho Cavalcante's marketing efforts in Salvador da Bahia. Gonçalo's academy would become a big success in future years and into the Internet Age.

Returning to the "feira:" there were many stands selling clothing, others with meat cooked on a spit ["churrasquinho no espeto"] and literally dozens of beer stands. It is Sunday morning entertainment for the northeasterners in Rio, their option instead of the beach at Copacabana, Leblon or Ipanema. The noise level was abominable and it was impossible to have a decent conversation with Gonçalo. I hopped a bus back to the hotel but would have stayed longer in the fair except for the exhaustion of the long overnight flight to Rio.

Miscellaneous moments of the day in Rio

I took a shower and ate the rest of the "snacks" from the flight: apple, crackers, chocolate and cheese from Varig. Now dressed in walking shorts, tennis shoes and t-shirt I took bus 154 to Ipanema and the Hippy Fair; it seemed huge, bigger than before. It was great for leather objects, wood carvings (colored macaws, huge and heavy), costume jewelry, and colored glass scenes by the same artist as in 1985 (landmarks of Rio, toucans, and parrots). I searched for the leather map artist Glauco, found him and a wonderful depiction of a caravel on the high sea; I lost the opportunity to buy it because of not having enough cash with me. When I returned with "cruzados" it had been sold, but all was not lost: I bought a beautiful leather representation of the tall ship "The Cutty Sark" on the high sea.

The streets were full of people and cars and I noted more poor people in Copacabana, Ipanema and Leblon; the times are changing. I saw so much I wanted to buy in the Hippy Fair, but it was just not possible, both for the cost of it all and for the lack of room in luggage and the problem of getting it on the airplane. On the other hand, Keah and I had made some nice purchases back in 1985 at the same spot.

Lunch was fine at an orange juice stand.

Then came a long stroll on the "calçada" or sidewalk along Ipanema Beach; the street along the beach is now closed to traffic on Sunday and is delightful with passersby and bicyclists like along the "aterro" in Flamengo. The result is the beaches and sidewalks are turned into real parks; the system has been in effect for two years now. There were many people on the beach but it was not jammed like on those hot summer days in Rio. I really wanted to go for a dip but it was not feasible this time. There was electoral propaganda everywhere either for Lula and running mate Covas; it was like a parade and the atmosphere was entertaining, much like the speeches I heard on television that night.

Hungry, I ate a really good "canja de galinha – com arroz, galinha e cenoura" plus a cold beer; the price was right, about $3USD. It was a good lunch for the gringo's fragile stomach at the time. There was time for a calm "cafezinho" in front of the Hippy Fair in Ipanema, but I was alone!

The return to the hotel via Copacabana was as in 1988; I did not feel out of place in walking shorts since it was Sunday and a beach day. I got off the bus a little early to walk through Flamengo; it was pretty along the beach but I felt a little uncomfortable in the interior streets, standing out I'm sure from afar as a "gringo." The Hotel Novo Mundo is being remodeled (thus all the noise I complained of earlier); they are redoing the lobby and bringing computerization. One result for sure will be higher prices.

I telephoned old friend Henrique Kerti (remember there are no cell phones yet for anybody); I'll see them Tuesday night for dinner, the night before the big election.

Tomorrow I'll go to the Rui Barbosa Foundation to look at the "cordel" collection and see old colleagues; the nearby National Institute of Folklore with its "cordel" collection is closed – on strike!

The next morning there was a good breakfast in the calm dining room of the Hotel Novo Mundo: orange juice, pineapple, watermelon, good French bread, scrambled eggs and a fine "café com leite." For curiosity seekers, the hotel's tariff was $32 USD per day.

I got on the wrong bus for Botafogo and the "Casa de Rui" so I had to walk about fifteen minutes; call it "Getting to Know Botafogo." It is sunny and hot today.

The Director of the Research Center Homero Senna is on vacation. I went to the library and had complete access to the "cordel" collection. Thus began a somewhat frantic search for the best story-poems, checking out once again the originals of Leandro Gomes de Barros, too fragile to Xerox, but one might recall that I had hand written note cards on his entire works done painstakingly back in 1966 and 1967. An Aside: years later the entire Gomes de Barros collection would be digitalized and made available "to the world" by researchers headed by Ivone Maia whom I would correspond with and meet years later in João Pessoa. So while looking for story-poems of documentary or historic themes (this was research for the major book published later at the University in São Paulo in 1998), one of the librarians came up and said, "Professor, I have lamentable news for you! The 'Fundação Casa de Rui Barbosa' is going to go on strike at noon." You can imagine my reaction – traveling 4000 miles for this research and facing a strike! Being the good Brazilians they are, they took pity on me and allowed me to actually take a couple of dozen story-poems outside "to the street" for Xeroxing, all to be done before noon. There followed a tense short lunch while quickly perusing the story-poems, choosing the ones for Xeroxing and then facing a monumental battle with Brazilian bureaucracy (the guy in charge of the Xerox machine at the Foundation). By three o'clock that p.m. I had fifteen to twenty excellent story-poems Xeroxed for the future book. Many a colleague of research in Brazil will nod his/her head in agreement with the small adventure.

At Orígenes Lessa's library with hostess Maria Eduarda Lessa

Curran at the library of Orígenes Lessa at his home

Maria Eduarda Lessa allows me to see Orígenes' "cordel" collection, but I cannot take any story-poems out to the street to Xerox. It becomes like 1966 when all my notes were hand written on file cards! But the research can still be accomplished (recall that the National Institute of Folklore is also on strike). Everything turned out well: Maria Eduardo changed her mind and let me take "folhetos" to a nearby Xerox machine on the street. The result was many fine story-poems Xeroxed, all necessary for the future book.

Another day, the trolley to Santa Teresa and the "Casa de São Saruê" with Umberto Peregrino and other moments

It was an interesting day that would begin with breakfast in the hotel, subway to the "Largo do Carioca" passing by the Petrobras Building and the New Cathedral. Then I caught the old electric trolley car (the same as that of the famous film "Black Orpheus" ["Orféu Negro"]) to Santa Teresa. It was old and worn but provided an incredible view of the "Baia de Guanabara." I do not recommend it for those fearful of assault and muggings! The passengers were all black, I the "White cat in a field of blackness," paraphrasing Érico Veríssimo and his "Gato Preto em Campo de Neve," the story of his diplomatic days in Washington D.C. in the 1940s. It was a thrill to hang on to the streetcar's ceiling straps while passing over the Lapa Aqueduct!

I went to Santa Teresa to finally meet General Umberto Peregrino who lived in an old colonial mansion with a large garden; he renamed the place "Casa de São Saruê" (an obvious homage to the famous poet of "cordel" Manoel Camilo dos Santos of Paraíba, incidentally interviewed by me in 1966 and appearing in my first book "A Literatura de Cordel" by the University of Pernambuco Press in 1973). It is a private folklore center with tropical birds in the garden and fine artisan products of the old Northeast. When Umberto was young he was a student of Luís da Câmara Cascudo, my adviser of "cordel" in Rio Grande do Norte State in 1966, and he was a cadet in the Military College with Manuel Cavalcanti Proença my first adviser of studies in Rio in 1966. Umberto and his wife Artis were very kind to me. In his museum he has the original printing press of the "cordel" poet, woodcut artist Dila of Caruaru, and the entire collection of the iconoclastic "cordel" poet from Rio, Raimundo Santa Helena. In the 1960s Umberto was the President-Director of the National Institute of the Book ["Instituto Nacional do Livro"] the most important government publishing entity in Brazil.

To the side of the Museum there was a small building with modest rooms for lodging itinerant poets and folklore scholars who come to Rio; Rodolfo Coelho Cavalcante of Salvador, Bahia, was a frequent guest as was Franklin Machado of São Paulo. Umberto spoke of "cordel" and the Northeast; he publishes occasional "folhetos" for local poets, these of very high quality. He allowed me to peruse the entire "cordel" collection and I was able to take away on hand written note cards about 40 story-poems, many of which would appear in the future book at the USP in São Paulo in 1998. I said to myself: "You have to come back again and next time bring your camera and take photos of this place!" Incidentally Umberto has a large cassette tape collection of Northeastern music.

Lunch was folkloric; Umberto had arranged lunch for me in the annex of the local police station in the area. "If I survive, we will celebrate: rice, black beans, a leg of chicken, onions, but in doubtful circumstances." I spoke to one of the employees (was he from the Northeast?) and understood perhaps every fifth word out of his mouth.

Upon returning to the "Casa de São Saruê" we were greeted by a duet of two "seresteiro" singers; they were great and I felt at home.

I returned to the city on the aforementioned street car. It was right out of "Black Orpheus," riding the rails on top of the Lapa Aqueduct, the trolley was jammed pack with passengers, all black once again. Some students told me later that "this was a very dangerous place."

In sum, as to the "Casa de São Saruê," it was difficult to get there to say the least. Umberto had asked me to give talks there at an indefinite time in the future; the audience would be high school students the professors send there to "study folklore." In all humility I am a bit surprised to realize how much I do know about Brazilian Folklore at this stage of the academic career, of the "cordel" and Brazil in general, and with the perspective gained from all these years of study and field work. They say that "cordel" is now in all the primary schools and high schools as "popular communication." In spite of my nervousness the trip to São Saruê was incredible with its view of Rio, downtown and the Bay of Guanabara.

An Aside: the subway! It was extremely quiet with no graffiti and good air conditioning in the cars and in the stations. It was something to admire. But outside the subway the walls of the local buildings were full of graffiti.

There was another surprise: on the return trip home to the hotel in Flamengo the doors of the Catete Palace ["Palácio do Catete"] were open (it was supposed to be closed for remodeling). Built in 1858 in an imitation of the Rococo style, it was the first presidential palace of the Republic. Its greatest claim to fame was that President Getúlio Vargas committed suicide there in 1954. Restored, it was indeed beautiful but unfortunately there were no post cards for sale, no tourist brochures or posters, just the memories! It is one of the important places to see in Brazil for anyone interested in the country's political history.

Another Aside. There are notices on television to NOT vote for those candidates with noisy advertising or those who have taken down the posters of other candidates in the streets. Another unrelated note on the TV: topless ads are now common, quite a change from the old days of the military dictatorship and its goal of a return to morality and family values. Perhaps because of the construction in the hotel, the "pum, pum, pum" of the hammers, it all was a bit uncomfortable. Tomorrow is Election Day and the promised meeting with my friends the Kertis.

An economic note of the day: interest rates in a bank savings account are 50 per cent per month. True inflation for the last calendar year passed 1000 per cent! The main investment vehicle to preserve savings and capital, the "Overnight" is at a whopping 29 per cent!

That same day I caught the metro and went to the Largo do Machado where I met Gonçalo Ferreira da Silva (I had seen him briefly at the São Cristóvão Fair yesterday but it was too noisy to talk). We were able to have a nice conversation and Gonçalo will be a good "cordel" connection in the future - there will be an ironic surprise when we meet again in Washington D.C. in 2010 in the symposium of the Folklife Center of the U.S. Library of Congress. Back at the Largo do Machado we had "cafezinho" in the same bar where I met the great "cordel" poet Azulão (João José dos Santos) in December of 1966 and where I saw "Bumba Meu Boi" for the first time in Brazil. This was twenty-two years ago!

The next day was Wednesday and it was Election Day. I went back to the Lessa's apartment where I would continue to read "folhetos" from Orígenes' amazing collection;

it was difficult in the good sense because there is an enormous amount of quality story-poems for my future book.

Another day, an encounter with Adriano da Gama Kury at the Casa de Rui Barbosa Foundation

Once again I was with Adriano da Gama Kury of the Research Center of the Casa de Rui Barbosa Foundation. He is almost totally deaf now but is still an active researcher with a new Brazilian Grammar Book, a best seller of its kind in Brazil!

Back in the hotel I thought I was going crazy hearing the sound of tropical birds, parakeets and small parrots. It turns out it is common for people to keep them in cages in the inside balconies of the hotel. Old-timers will recall such a custom in Orpheus' house in the Babylonia "favela" in the movie.

A new encounter with my friends the Kertis at the Glória Hotel

Henrique, Cristina, Letícia and friends, Rio, 1989

Curran and the Kertis

That night Henrique and Cristina Kerti picked me up at the hotel at 9:30 p.m. for dinner. Henrique has a cast on his foot due to slipping at work a month ago; he works in Novo Friburgo at a packing plant, a connection to Cristina's family. He commutes 50 kilometers each day on the Via Dutra the main Rio de Janeiro – São Paulo highway. He hopes to retire at the age of 52; he is 46 now. The idea is to maintain a small apartment in Rio and a quieter place outside the city. Money is not a problem, but things are more difficult now. A trip to Europe or the United States or even Paraguay for Carnival is possible once in a while. He has no hobbies but hopes to start some after he retires. Cristina likes gardening and getting out of the house. Due to an operation for throat cancer she is permanently "hoarse" now. Henrique is much the same; he is overweight, still smokes and likes Black and White Scotch. Letícia is in sixth grade and is currently doing a project on the ocean (this made me think of our daughter Katie and her Science Fairs; she is the same age as Letícia).

The Kertis at the Hotel Glória

Time for confession

Mark and Henrique Kerti, the Hotel Glória, 1989

Mark and the portrait of Emperor Pedro II, Hotel Glória, 1989

Due to election day the maid has the day off so we have to go out to eat dinner. We ended up at the restaurant of the Hotel Glória at 10:30 p.m., dining alone in the formal dining room. There was good conversation and we spoke of everything – the children, the days at Rockhurst College in Kansas City, Missouri, hotels, the cost of travel (they are going to Paraguay for Carnival; the hotel has a casino and the guests never leave the hotel).

We noted that Cristina's new car has an alarm for thieves. See the good photos of the "colonial" rooms in the hotel; they are funny, including Cristina hearing Mark's confession! The portrait of Dom Pedro II is a good memory.

The dinner was elegant, the main course $7.50 USD which would be at least $20 in the US. (remember: this is 1989). An economic note: Brazilians pay by personal bank check when eating out. Henrique wanted to know how much it would cost to rent an RV for a trip in the United States, a bit of a whim I think. Perhaps I'll see them again when he retires, but not before. He wants Keah and me to come to Brazil, to bring Katie so she can meet Letícia. He believes language will not be a problem, even though Letícia speaks little English and Katie no Portuguese. Why? Because Henrique arrived in the United States to study at Rockhurst knowing zero English and remembers the experience.

The Colonial Room in the Hotel Glória still is one of the prettiest in Rio, little changed from my time there for that conference in 1973, but the hotel is totally restored. The neighborhood is not doing all that well. However the hotel does sport a new escalator!

I'm back at my digs, the Novo Mundo, at midnight and still do not sleep well.

Another day, once again with Maria Eduarda Lessa, reading the "Orígenes Lessa 'Cordel' Collection"

It's election day and is beautiful weather. The Cariocas vote and then go to the beach; it is difficult to write these notes with all the noise outside – the blaring horns of cars, political parades and the view of Copacabana in the distance. I had a great breakfast; could it be I am gaining weight (something totally new for this "gringo")? I took a bus to Maria Eduarda's house at ten a.m. and worked until about 4:30. I took her the presents Keah helped me pick out in Arizona, nice Southwestern U.S. souvenirs. Maria Eduarda says, and I can't count on this, that my study "Grande Sertão: Veredas e a Literatura de Cordel" may still perhaps come out in a joint publication with the "Biblioteca Lençóis Paulista" and "José Olympio Editoral." She says we will know more at the beginning of next year. "It's a matter of honor," she says (the agreement of the library with Orígenes himself). I thought to myself: I've waited this long; what's one more year?

Maria Eduarda's father was a general in the Portuguese Army in Angola before Independence; he died just two months after Orígenes death. The rest of the family is in Lisbon; they happen to have a house in Sintra. I told of our trip to Portugal and we reminisced of the beauty of Sintra.

We spoke of the good days while Orígenes was alive and my visits with them – the "cafezinhos" and honey from the farm mixed with lemon juice. I bought lunch for us that day – Mark's lunch to be sure – "galeto, batata frita, molho à campanha." I think it was a good moment for the two of us, Maria Eduarda and I. A research note: I copied on note cards the bibliography of the entire collection of political story-poems in Orígenes' collection. If all goes well I'll Xerox the important "folhetos" tomorrow morning. What confidence and trust Maria has had in me! If I accomplish all this I will be well on the road to a good research article or even a book (that turned to be the one at the EDUSP in 1998). And thus the research time in Rio will be a success!

The Casa de Rui Barbosa Foundation is still on strike; I'll remember this possibility if I come to Brazil next year. After the Lessas it was back to the Hotel Novo Mundo. There was a sign in the street: "As you nose goes, so goes the country." ["Como vai o nariz; assim vai o país"]. "He who can smell votes for Gabeira" ["Quem cheira, vote em Gabeira"]. There was a carnival atmosphere on the bus home and all the black kids carrying on. It was a historic day for me: I saw the same happiness and festive spirit on the streets as in the "old days" before the dictatorship; the "carioca" spirit is alive and well. The plan is to organize my research thus far, have lunch in the "confeitaria" near the hotel and return to the room to see the election results on the TV. Right now I'm fresh out of social contacts; on the other hand there is time to do these notes; without them there will be no book!

The next day I'm dragging my body down to breakfast after a very fitful night of sleep. I caught a bus to Maria Eduarda's house and after a few technical difficulties, I Xeroxed almost two volumes of old "folhetos" which make a success of this research period in Rio! The material weighs a lot and will mean full bags for the return trip home. An Aside: "TV Educação" is great! It saves me some idle hours in Brazil; there are no commercials and there are good documentary clips of Brazil; it is much akin to PBS at home.

I changed some travelers' checks in a tourist agency to pay the hotel bill; the exchange being better than that of the hotel. I checked out the price for the Hotel Toledo (2-3 stars) in Copacabana and will move there tomorrow so I can be close to the beach for a couple of days.

The following two days were pretty busy – I had a fish dinner at Maria Eduarda's, done especially for me by Aparecida the maid. I want to go to Copacabana Beach Saturday morning; I deserve it!

A Note: If one keeps his eyes open he will notice all the people living in the streets all over the city. Life does go on. For me the routine was much the same: the big meal today was "galeto, molho à campanha, arroz à grega, cerveja e cafezinho," my favorite! I hope to get together with Ivan Cavalcanti Proença and perhaps Luís Raimundo Fernandes, a friend from 1981 in Salvador, now married and living in Rio. I have a bad cold and am very stuffed up, am taking Vitamin C and perhaps Ampicillin if it gets worse. I had a terrible night with the cold, am I dying?

I slept better than the last three nights, but I still feel sick. I had breakfast at the Hotel Novo Mundo and left for a new 3 star hotel with a swimming pool. Bye-Bye Novo Mundo! The taxi was two dollars US to the new hotel. The bad news: there is no room with a view of the ocean; you only get that on the top floor. The good news: the daily rate is USD $16 and the room is nicer than that at the Novo Mundo. The hotel is only one block from the beach, two blocks from the Post Office and is very comfortable, although a lot noisier.

I walked to Maria Eduarda's house, and note, I *finished* the review of Orígenes' vast collection; I found five or six more old and good story-poems to Xerox. We had a lunch of "badejo, abacaxi e mate." On the return walk to the hotel I walked along Copacabana Beach ("Wish you were here Keah"). Then I got things organized for the trip north, a rather large task in itself. I will leave all the books and the mounds of Xeroxed copies in the locker in the airport. It is my last night in Rio.

On the TV the old time politician Leonel Brizola (see the notes from previous books back to the 1960s, the Left and the Military Dictatorship), as is his custom, is protesting the election results. He says that the TV cheated on its coverage of his campaign and it was really all fraud.

The Research. I felt very satisfied over the work done in Rio; I did the maximum possible under the circumstances and I have a lot of good new material. I hope to acquire more, especially in João Pessoa.

For the time being I will not have to deal with Carlos Cunha and the question of publications in Salvador, Bahia. Maria Eduarda is optimistic that "Grande Sertão: Veredas e a Literatura de Cordel" will come out in a co-edition with the library in Lençóis Paulista after the beginning of the New Year.

The cold remedy or just the passing of time has had a good effect; I finally feel better from that nasty cold.

I have an appointment tomorrow with Ivan Cavalcanti Proença. He is the son of Manuel Cavalcanti Proença, my first advisor of studies in Brazil in 1966 while on the Fulbright Grant, short-lived to be sure. The reader of Volume I of "Peripécias" will recall my shock in Rio in December of 1966 while watching the evening news at the Kertis house – the funeral resulting from the death of Manuel Cavalcanti Proença! I was not only astounded but left high and dry for research for the rest of that year in Brazil. It all turned out well, but I did not know that then.

I am homesick for my family in Arizona. How is Keah doing? And Katie – school and violin? Football at ASU? One third of my trip is finished.

Another day, an encounter with Ivan Cavalcanti Proença and other moments

The good and the bad. I was very well received in Ivan's home in Flamengo. He is a fan of the Blues and has been to New Orleans. I spoke of you, Keah, and of your ability to catch all the lyrics of the Black Blues singers (as opposed to me with the "bum" ears). Frankly, Proença controlled the moment and the conversation: he spoke of Doris Turner, my first professor of Portuguese and Brazilian Literature, now a professor at Kent State (Ivan visited her there). Ivan seems incredibly busy. He was not particularly helpful with answers to my questions but did offer me the chance to peruse his "cordel" collection later on.

An Aside. He was the director of José Olympio Publishing Company when the Casa de Rui Barbosa originally sent my study on "cordel" and João Guimarães Rosa to be published. He left when Xerox purchased José Olympio. We did not talk of my study; there was nothing to be gained. And he wanted to speak of other things.

Moving on. My day at the beach never happened; it was cloudy with intermittent rain. I had to be satisfied with just a long walk along the "calçada" or mosaic sidewalk along the beach. It was disappointing to not be able to see any of those famous Carioca beauties in their entire splendor. So it all turned out okay; I was really too fatigued from the lack of sleep and the bad cold days earlier to be jousting with the waves at Copacabana. I made a few purchases in the shops on "Avenida Nossa Senhora de Copacabana," mainly humorous t-shirts, and Xeroxed the lyrics from the covers of several Chico Buarque de Holanda and Antônio Carlos Jobim albums. It was on this trip that I bought the Nativity Set made of diminutive "bonecos de barro" from Brazil's Northeast.

I had to repack my bags; the extra "Tiger" bag I bought is jammed with research material and gifts wrapped in dirty laundry. It will stay here in the luggage deposit of the hotel until my return from João Pessoa the last day of the trip.

Mark and Friend Luís Raimundo Fernandes, Rio

Tonight I'm going to Luís Raimundo Fernandes' house, an old friend from the boarding house days in Ondina in Salvador on one of the old research trips. He lives at the end of Leblon in the Gávea district. He is now married with a small child; we will trade photos of our wives and kids and reminisce a bit of Salvador days.

I wrote: "Rio would be great if you were here."

From Rio to Bahia, a return to the old "hangouts"

The taxi ride was in the a.m. passing by the "Lagoa" and the "Túnel Rebouças." Upon arriving at the airport in Salvador there was a long line of waiting in that tropical heat. It's hot! I stayed at the Barra Turismo Hotel in front of the beach of the same name, $20 USD per night. The air conditioning is marginal; twenty minutes out on the street here and you need another shower.

The next day the 20th of November was a busy one; it started with the "ônibus seletivo," like the "frescão" in Rio but without air conditioning. The Cultural Foundation of the State of Bahia and the "Núcleo for Research of the 'Cordel'" were closed in the morning. A bit later I walked to the Pelourinho and to the Jorge Amado Foundation where Edilene Matos is now an assistant to Myriam Fraga the director. It is a great place, of high quality; I saw all the excellent photos of Jorge in the showcases including the books for study of his works. For tourism's sake I purchased a couple of the Exú T-Shirts as souvenirs.

There was a brief visit to the "Church of the Third Order" ["Igreja da Terceira Ordem"] to the side of the famous Church of São Francisco. The Portuguese blue tiles inside the Third Order were wonderful but seemed neo-classical in style; the façade is like Spanish Baroque (I've spoken of it many times and with photos from past trips). Many armed police were in evidence, and the area still seemed old, dirty and poor (the remodeling of the Pelourinho area had not yet taken place; today in 2016 it presents a far better appearance).

A taxi took me to "A Portuguesa," the restaurant from my boarding house in 1966. Everyone is still there – old Carmina the one really in charge, her daughter Miquelina, working and "slaving away" and still commanding the kitchen, Amândio the bar man. One enjoys their incredible "daily special:" soup, macaroni, rice, beans with real ham, a very large portion of roasted chicken, fruit salad and "cafezinho," all for a total of $3.90 USD.

I returned to the "Núcleo" and it was depressing; I consulted what was left of the entire collection and found perhaps ten story-poems useful for the research. It was as they say in Brazil "um desleixo geral" ["a big mess"]. Perhaps the reason is that Edilene Matos, its former director, left the Cultural Foundation of the State of Bahia and is now teaching three classes at the Federal University of Bahia at night and has returned to the Foundation as head of the Literature Section only a month ago. She is at the Jorge Amado Foundation in the morning, the State Cultural Foundation in the afternoon and teaches at night. There were "good vibes" being with Carlos and Edilene once again.

An Interesting Professional Aside: Carlos and I found my manuscript on the poet Cuíca de Santo Amaro in a desk drawer of the Cultural Foundation gathering dust. I pulled it at once. Cunha admits that "cordel" is a difficult theme or topic for publication in Bahia now. So the cliché became true: "It's in the drawer" ["Está na gaveta"].

A new encounter with Carlos Cunha and Edilene Matos and the news about "cordel"

Carlos Cunha, Edilene Matos, Salvador, 1989

We gathered at Cunha's house that night. Carol is now fourteen years old and about as tall as our daughter Katie. They have remodeled the patio; it is now replete with coconut trees and macaws! Their house is like an art museum.

Carlos gets all excited when talking about "cordel" with me; he says there is no one in Salvador these days with the same interest or panoramic view of the same. The journalist Marconi may yet do a book on Cuíca de Santo Amaro. Carlos and Edilene were impressed with my book of 1987: "A Presença de Rodolfo Coelho Cavalcante na Moderna Literatura de Cordel" (Nova Fronteira, Rio), and the bilingual anthology on "cordel" in Madrid in 1990. The summary of the question of publication in Bahia is as follows: I have nothing to lose or gain so I can just relax.

I telephoned my research colleague and host in João Pessoa, Neuma Fechine Borges, who informed me a small seminar on "cordel" was cancelled because I could not be there, but is now scheduled anew. I am programmed to speak for fifty minutes on the first day. The only outside guests are Roberto Benjamin (U. of Recife) and myself, but the local scholars are excellent. Neuma and her husband are going to drive me to Campina Grande on the weekend so I can finally meet Átila de Almeida.

Recalling Bahia: the ocean was beautiful but it seems like there are thousands of poor in and on the streets and poverty seems to be growing. Life is good in Brazil if you have money.

As to research there is nothing new under the sun now in Bahia; there's no point ["está sem graça"] to return to the Cultural Foundation or the "Núcleo" of Research on "cordel." My old friend Mário Barros is in São Paulo but I did get to talk by phone with his wife Laís.

Another day, getting around Salvador

I caught a taxi to the Lower City and went to the old poetry stand of Rodolfo Coelho Cavalcante in front of the Modelo Market. It was sad. I met one of his sons, Rodolfo Júnior I think; they had received my package of books some time back with the copies of my big book on Rodolfo. They thanked me; I found perhaps ten useful "folhetos" from the poetry stand, so if you add these to the few from the "Núcleo" it was not all a waste of time.

"I'm at loose ends with time on my hands and not much to do."

Barra Beach, Salvador, 1989

On another day I had a great swim at my old favorite Barra Beach and then packed my bags for João Pessoa. I had a last lunch with Carlos and Edilene followed with a visit with Carlos at the Academy of Letters. It was at this point that there was a big surprise: a sudden "lightening" bus strike ["greve de relâmpago"], no taxis in the area and me now in a terrific hurry to get to the airport. It continued with a long walk searching for a taxi, finally finding one and a wild and crazy ride to the airport.

Returning to the bus strike: I can literally not express the panic and concern I felt when I found out about the strike; I have no idea how far I walked, half lost in that part of the city and no taxi to be seen. I was surrounded by what seemed like thousands of "bahianos" in the same predicament and time passing.

Arriving in João Pessoa and Neuma Fechine Borges

It was a good flight; Neuma and José Elias Borges were waiting for me at the airport, and then took me to a modest hotel but very close to Manaíra Beach with all its activity. We actually arrived at the hotel at 2:30 a.m.; this is the sort of thing one needs to remember: the incredibly Brazilian hospitality in such situations. I think it would not be the same at home in the good ole' USA. The modest hotel was fine, the food tasty (if you are not eating alone); it is located one long block from the beach – a crescent of palm trees, but the sea with muddy water. It gave me "saudades" of that nice clean, blue-green water from Barra Beach in Salvador, my favorite from years back.

Neuma is great! A sincere and honest host! At this point in 1989 she has her Master's but not a doctorate, and there are some in the university that do not let her forget the latter, but she is highly respected. (Times are going to change for her, at least in the academic sense, when she "reigned" over the congress on "cordel" in João Pessoa in 2005, now with the Ph.D. and honorific degree from Portiers!)

The seminar, the presentation, and dinner with Idelette Mozart

The Seminar. The auditorium is full to capacity with people sitting on the steps, but there is no air conditioning and it is very hot. I was the first to talk, the invited guest and "featured speaker" of that day. The presentation went very well, in fact in an excellent manner; the public and the students liked it and my Portuguese went fine. The "debate" that followed was not quite the same – it was difficult – it seemed that all the questions were coming from Literary Criticism and Theory people. I think I defended myself as best I could; I am not of that "persuasion" – Literary Theory. On the other hand, I am a "number 10" on matters of "cordel," past, present and future. It turns out today, 1989, the "master and commander" in the universities at such conferences is the theoretical approach which by the way my friend and mentor Orígenes Lessa deplored (perhaps for this reason liking me and giving me so much encouragement and support). The fact he was an original writer of fiction and really had a low opinion of literary critics (the cliché: "Those that can't write, critique.") might be a related issue. Back to "cordel:" what was clear is that I got there first and was a real "pioneer" in "cordel" research. Neuma told me later that the debate was a sort of "setup," meant to be "political" in nature – her enemies had as its purpose to make me look bad, thus "wounding" my hostess and guide as well. I have heard of such academic nonsense since then (most recently in an account by a naturalist-scientist-researcher on the National Geographic Explorer of his experience at universities in the 1980s) but had never encountered it before. Or perhaps I was too naïve to realize what was happening in front of my eyes!

An Aside: There was a talk about racial prejudice in the "cordel," and it was very uncomfortable for me, showing a racial prejudice still prevalent and strong in the Northeast. It was a good thing the "gringo" did not give that talk, a "gringo" from the land of racial prejudice!

An intellectual "super star" was present – Idelette Mozart Fonseca, French ancestry, titles of Master's Degree and Ph.D. from the Sorbonne – her dissertation was the first from the Sorbonne dealing with the theme of Brazilian folk-popular poetry and was directed by Raymund Cantel. As to the debates discussed previously, I wrote: "I think she tried to put me over a barrel, but I jumped out"! I would really be more relaxed and in a better mental state the next day of the conference with presentations from people from popular communications, not the literary people, folks like Roberto Benjamin.

That morning was followed by the big Brazilian mid-day meal and more talks that afternoon – a little boring for me but necessary. It was extremely hot; I think I took four showers that day! I had dinner that night with Idelette and her husband João Luís. She told me that in the beginning of her academic career she was directed to meet two people: Raymund Cantel and Mark Curran and that she was very happy to finally have contact with me. It was mutual. I found it odd that she, Neuma or Edilene Matos had never met or been in touch with Candace Slater, research colleague from Stanford and later Berkeley, but they know of her work.

An Aside: My approach to the "cordel" according to theme and content is now passé and seems "invalid" for those in Literature ["Letras"] today. The irony of this: all would change years later with the book "História do Brasil em Cordel" at the USP in São Paulo in 1998! My thesis was proved! So the question at that moment at the University in João Pessoa was: either sophisticated literary theory with its mysterious terminology would win or old-fashioned direct talk and common sense! I wished I had had Orígenes there to defend me! But they still search me out; they cannot deny I have come so far in the past with research and I have met so many important writers and poets, many now gone. Anyway, Idelette was very pleasant in her visit with me.

Another day, the seminar and the many presentations

This morning I feel a bit worn out due to a lack of sleeping well. I did like a couple of the talks. I hear and understand everything when it is calm, but when they turn on the loud fans or speak without microphones I miss most of it. I've taken aspirin this trip, stress headaches I think. The talks that day provided one of interest by a professor from the University of Paraíba in Campina Grande. Roberto Benjamin was good but I thought to myself: "He's playing the same old record." In the Brazilian academic milieu one is successful by "presence," meeting others, spending time with others and networking. Others tell me that Roberto Benjamin is a wealthy man from the sugar cane industry in Pernambuco; he chooses to participate in the Academy because he does not need to do anything else. Gossip. Who knows!

There is the large mid-day meal in the hotel: fish and shrimp, both very tasty. The television is on at maximum volume, the dining room is full, has echoes, and everyone seems to be talking. It was difficult for the "gringo," but I did manage to "get" most of Roberto Benjamin's conversation. His talk that morning was a revelation for me: a videotape of Edson Pinto and Olegário Fernandes in Caruaru reciting "The Death of Luís Gonzaga" ["A Morte de Lus Gonzaga"]. Benjamin lives in a remodeled colonial mansion on the Rua da Aurora in Recife and teaches at the "Universidade Rural Pernambucana."

Current news: Ariano Suassuna has just been elected to the Brazilian Academy of Letters in Rio de Janeiro but is refusing to make the journey to the big city to participate in the ceremony and accept the honor. This is one more case of the tradition of intellectual provincialism in Brazil, especially the Northeast. His fame is due amazingly enough to one small play – "The Rogues' Trial" ["O Auto da Compadecida"] based mainly on three classics of old "cordel" by the great poet Leandro Gomes de Barros, a play that was an entire chapter in my Ph.D. dissertation in 1968. I found out later that that was just the beginning; there was much more going on than my early connection to him: his life and fame as a professor of aesthetics at the Federal University in Pernambuco, the cultural movement he founded in Recife: "The Armorial Movement" ["O Movimento Armorial"] and his now famous "class spectacles" ["aulas espetáculos"], the latter broadcast on national TV and known to all. I recall a film that I had seen years later after 1989; it dealt with Rio de Janeiro and Carnival and Ariano was the theme of one of the famous samba schools and seen riding on their float in the big parade. Aside from all this, he always treated me well, with politeness, consideration and respect.

I wrote these notes to Keah in English: "Please put up with me; these are reflections on an entire career with many emotions as you shall see." Today I was very frustrated at the conference: twenty-five years of dealing with "cordel," a plethora of observations, facts and bits of knowledge and with no way to share it in those moments. Déjà vu: I don't believe they are aware of all I knew, I know and what I have done. So much of what they talk of is as if it were new, stuff I already knew and had published studies on it; the worst is that they don't know that I know! Pardon the "outburst," just emotional musings at the time. (Am I getting to be an "old crank?")

It was a frustrating afternoon: Átila de Almeida in Campina Grande is sick. It won't be possible to be with him, therefore there will be no trip to Campina Grande and consequently no way to see his "cordel" collection. I tried hard this p.m. to change the airline reservations and leave for home on the 26th. It turns out there are no available seats on the plane until December 2nd. Better to leave things the way they are.

I was not feeling so well that p.m. but was obliged to keep my word and dine with Professor Maurice Van Woesen, a former Catholic Priest from Belgium who came to Brazil in 1962. He left the priesthood, got married and has a very successful family. They were all wonderful with me; he works on the medieval themes and relation to "cordel," that is, the "Chanson de Roland." He did his Master's Thesis on Ariano Suassuna. His wife is a social worker in the town of Santa Rita fifty kilometers from João Pessoa. There is one family that owns all the land in the region, harking back to feudal times in Europe! Catholic priests are considered "dangerous" because of the current theological "preference for the poor." I did not regret our time together.

Miscellaneous moments from João Pessoa

I slept eight hours last night and that helped a lot. There was a visit to the "Cordel Poetic Library of the Federal University of Paraiba" ["A Biblioteca de Poesia de Cordel da Universidade Federal de Paraíba"] with Neuma and I found some twenty story-poems and was able to Xerox them. There was lunch of filet and then a nap and then a swim at Manaíra Beach with beautiful waves. Keah and Katie I wish you were here!

In free moments I am working frantically to cut the manuscript of my book on Cuíca de Santo Amaro for publishing in Salvador; there are already one hundred pages cut.

And there was an opportunity to play the guitar and sing by the pool in the hotel, all good except for one inebriated person at the pool. Then I got ready to go out with Neuma and José Elias later that day. We went to the famous "Cultural Space of João Pessoa" ["O Espaço Cultural de João Pessoa"]. It is gigantic: it features musical shows, theatrical productions, cinema and the José Lins do Rego Museum. The capacity is 20,000 persons; it is made of concrete and steel and the architectural plan is based on a building in Paris. I thought, "This and thousands of people dying of hunger in Brazil!" (Shades of the 2016 Olympics in Rio with all the brouhaha.)

Manaíra Beach, João Pessoa, 1989

"Keah, if we come to João Pessoa I know where we will stay." We went to Timbaú Beach, the "Ipanema" of João Pessoa and I saw its five star hotel: round like an old fort, all the rooms facing the sea, and there are beautiful gardens and hammocks strung outside each room. In front of the hotel there is a "hippie fair" and restaurants all providing an interesting atmosphere. The price in 1989 was $70 USD minus fifteen per cent if you have the air pass. The sea is another matter; it is not nearly as pretty as the ocean at Salvador or in Rio, but the waves are such one could body surf ["make like an alligator" or "fazer jacaré"]. Katie would love it. We ate chicken pizza and had cold beer at the beach. There was a lot of time spent with Neuma and José Elias. And there were many Brazilian beauties that afternoon on the beach.

On Sunday we did an outing to the "Praia das Seixas" or "Pebble Beach." It is the easternmost land point in the Americas! An Aside: Neuma was born near Crato in Ceará (recall my 1966 trip to the land of Padre Cícero seen in an earlier travel book); she was twelve years old when the family moved to Campina Grande, Paraiba, and her father became mayor of that city. It is a large family and she has sisters in Bahia, Fortaleza and the interior of the Northeast. Her politics is PT (the workers' party, later on of Lula fame), and her sister Neli has a Ph.D. in biochemistry from the Federal University of Paraiba. Both earn a good salary but there are momentous political battles going on within the university. (An Unnecessary Aside: today I received notice of the death of three colleagues from my early days at ASU, food for thought.)

About Átila de Almeida

Neuma spoke to me about Átila de Almeida. He is a first cousin of the famous José Américo de Almeida perhaps the most famous politician in the history of Paraíba State (I recall that in 1966 my contact and guide in Paraíba State, Professor Juárez Batista invited me to meet José Américo. Out of ignorance I declined the invitation thinking it was just "one more politician" a huge error on my part and also showing a bit of naiveté and political ignorance on my part.) José Américo was a minor novelist in the Northeast but with one famous title "Sugar Cane Slash"["A Bagaceira"], the story of the plantation life in those times. He also was governor of the State in 1930, also a federal senator and a candidate for President of Brazil in the same year, the family wealthy from sugar cane plantations. His mentor João Pessoa was assassinated, shot to death by a member of the Dantas family, a political clan in Paraíba during those days. Ariano Suassuna's father in those days was I think mayor of João Pessoa and an ally of the Dantas. Days later Ariano's father was assassinated by a knife wound in Rio de Janeiro. Ariano was born in 1927 and was traumatized his entire life by this event; he never forgot it. He was poor AND a Protestant in his formative years in Taperoá in the Paraíban interior. Later he would go to Law School in Recife and would never return to live in Paraiba. His book "Novel of the Rock of the Kingdom" ["Romance da Pedra do Reino"] tells the entire story.

Returning to Átila: he was a professor of Mathematics in the UFEPBII in Campina Grande. He inherited his collection of "cordel" from his father and enlarged upon it; the second edition of the "Dicionário" registers 13,000 story-poems and most are from his collection. At the moment he is receiving treatment for cancer. His wife is Dona Ruth and his daughter is Oriana (from the stories of Roland and the Twelve Knights of France). Átila has a fine, sharp sense of humor which is very evident even with his sickness. He has over two hundred "folhetos" from the Guajarina Press alone (these are the poems which deal with WWII in "cordel")! We agreed that I would visit in 1990 and consult the "cordel" collection.

The end of the time in João Pessoa and an airplane anecdote

I thanked Neuma and José Elias for all they did for me. Now I would move on to Salvador. It's at this time that Carlos Cunha gave me the idea of writing directly to Jorge Amado and informing him that I am willing to provide a subsidy of $2000 USD (it ended up being taken from the small inheritance I received at the death of my brother Jim and thus the book is dedicated to him) for my book to be published at the Jorge Amado Foundation in Salvador and asking Jorge to write the preface. Surprisingly and very soon I received an answer from him, a "yes," so all would get done at the Jorge Amado Foundation. Just one year later there was a fine author's night and autograph signing in Salvador. I do not know if I ever got around, thus far, to describe the veritable "odyssey" with all its details in the efforts to publish the book: all the negotiations with the Casa de Rui Barbosa Foundation in Rio de Janeiro, and later with Olívia Barradas at the Cultural Foundation of the State of Bahia, a true "heroic crossing" ["travessia"] through the Brazilian publishing houses and all their bureaucracy. I will write later of the publishing of the book, suffice to say that Jorge Amado's fine words in the preface mark one of the high points of the academic career.

As Aside: it was in the Salvador airport on this trip that I made, for me, the major purchase of the Kennedy tapestry of the "baianas" which decorates our family room yet today in Mesa, Arizona.

On the return from Salvador to Rio a Jesuit priest from Spain was seated beside me. He was old and quite deaf and had been seventeen years in Brazil but still spoke with the peninsular accent. He now lives in Baturité, Ceará State. He spoke almost shouting (because of the deafness?) and almost everyone on the airplane could hear him. He was railing about the box lunch served to all of us on the plane; he did eat any of it and said he wanted to save it for later. All of a sudden he shouted, "A black guy stole it." It turns out one of the stewards on the flight was black! Embarassing!

We had a conversation of sorts; I spoke of my studies in Brazil, the "Route of the Sanctuaries" Keah and I had seen in Spain, the Catholic Church in Brazil, and my support of Lula and agrarian reform. The old man was of an antiquated and old faith. He did not like Padre Leonardo Boff or the Theology of Liberation one bit (Boff was one of the leaders of the movement in Brazil), or the "church of the people." He was going to Rio to attend a conference on the "New Evangelization." In 1990 he would go to Rome for a retreat and then a trip to the Holy Land. He ended his tirade, the worst of all, shouting, "Lower class people are flying now and that black guy stole my lunch."

Once again In Rio, the last dinner with Henrique Kerti and the end of the trip

Upon arriving all the passengers were as usual in a terrific hurry to get their baggage from the overhead bins and get off the airplane. I caught the "frescão" to Figueiredo Magalhães and walked to the hotel. There was a big task ahead: remaking all my bags with the books and research materials from the trip (stored in the deposit of the hotel).

There was dinner at 9:30 that night at the Kertis (it would be the last time I would be with Henrique). I have these travel notes: "Henrique is tired and says he does not feel well. It would not surprise me if he were to fall down dead!" That spur of the moment thought turned true. It happened – heart attack and death (I only found out years later). Letícia their daughter was there that night with one of her girlfriends, the daughter of a lawyer friend Lourenço who happens to have a house in Angra dos Reis. He invited me to visit. It was a wonderful night of good drink, good food, and good conversation. I got to the hotel at 1:30 a.m. The next morning I was a "zombie" due to sleeping fitfully due to the noise of the Rio garbage trucks on the street outside the hotel during the night.

On the last day in Rio I was saved by the fact that the strike at the Ruy Barbosa Foundation was over, so I spent the entire day collecting and Xeroxing "folhetos." They were extremely kind to me, in fact all the Brazilians at the diverse research places were the same. The collection of "cordel" at the Rui Foundation is still the best I know of in Brazil, at least up to this date. There was a quick conversation with Homero Senna the Director of Research for the Foundation, and he seemed genuinely happy to see me. This was not the case with one of the founders of the Casa de Rui, Americo Lacombe, but perhaps this can be explained by the fact he was a very old man, and besides, "this is just another American researcher in Rio" (there is a plethora of them!). Homero insisted that I go back to José Olympio Publishing Company, tell them that the Biblioteca Orígenes Lessa in Lençóis Paulista has funding to publish my "Grande Sertão: Veredas e a Literatura de Cordel," (the study with the prize in 1985 and that great trip for Keah and me to Brazil, told in Volume II) and all José Olympio has to do is inform Lençóis of the cost to publish. I'll believe it if it happens. I also saw Maria Eduarda Lessa at the Foundation and thanked her again and said goodbye; she was great!

I had already checked out of the hotel room that a.m. I had left all the luggage in the "depósito" and pleaded with them for a place to take a shower before going to the airport; the "jeito" was the employees' bathroom to the side of the lobby, a folkloric place, but it got the job done ["quebrou o galho"]. Killing time I did a short walk on the "calçada" at Copacabana and on the return gave a short English class to the young man who controlled the safe deposit box or "cofre." He turned out to be a Jehovah's Witness, black, poor, but a good fellow with a wife and daughter (life is truly difficult in Brazil in

1989; he earns a pittance in the hotel, but it's a job!) His job: he is literally locked into a tiny room, perhaps six by six feet, and locked with a key, which is the "safe deposit box" for guests at the hotel. He sits and waits hours for them to come.

So the time passed and I caught a taxi to the Galeão International Airport with the crankiest taxi driver I've ever had in Brazil. After a while I quit trying to converse. So, in the end, it was the reading of many texts of "cordel" on this trip, Xeroxing the important ones, that enabled me to complete the material to do "História do Brasil em Cordel" (University Press of São Paulo, 1998), the result of a chance encounter at Brown University in 1994 where I read an entertaining paper heard by Sérgio Miceli the then President of the University Press. The seed for this my most successful book in Brazil was planted years back with the short trips to Brazil and digging into the "cordel' archives, a lot of hard work.

I surmise that the reader who may see this and read between the lines will see that this was not an easy trip nor particularly happy. There were some good moments to be sure, but a lot of loneliness, pressure and stress. I asked myself if it was worth the effort.

CHAPTER III

BRAZIL 1990. RESEARCH AND TOURISM

The flight and the first days in Rio

America West was on time as was the luggage and the shuttle to the international terminal and the short check-in line at Varig with maybe 20-25 passengers waiting. There was time to read "Treasure Island," thanks to my daughter Katie.

It's the international flight from Tokyo to Rio de Janeiro, a 747 which is totally packed. There was an empty seat to one side of me and a pretty Japanese-Brazilian girl to my right, but we really could not have a good conversation due to her tiny voice and the loud noise of the jet engines. There was the normal good on-board service of Varig, but no beef this time, but rather some Japanese dish. There is a difference of four hours in Rio from daylight savings time in Los Angeles and the flight is eleven hours.

It was pouring down rain when we arrived in Rio; I had the "red light" at customs, but once they took a quick look at the bags, all were approved. I caught the "frescão" to Copacabana, got off in the rain due to a mistake on my part of the correct stop and had to walk with bags in the downpour for four or five blocks to the Hotel Toledo. They had received my letter with reservation request so all was well. I exchanged dollars for "cruzados" nearby but was nervous on the return to the hotel with my pockets stuffed with Brazilian cash.

I made the necessary phone calls – to Carlos Cunha and Edilene Matos in Salvador and to Neuma Fechine Borges in João Pessoa and finally to Luís Raimundo Fernandes a young friend I had made in Salvador on a previous research trip and now living in Rio. I spent a very pleasant evening with him and his family, wife and young child; they will possibly go to the U.S. in 1991-1992. I went to bed at 2 a.m. and slept until 11:30, a great start for me in Brazil.

Next morning there was a long walk on the mosaic sidewalk of Copacabana and it was great to get the exercise. Later reading the Sunday newspaper I discovered a major news and economic item: there will be a new economic "package" by the Collor de Mello government, the infamous "Plano Cruzélia" and the value of the dollar is expected to go down. I then went to the Hippy Fair in Ipanema where the fine artist Glauco has a leather map with a Portuguese Caravel sailing ship I am lusting after. The price is $54 USD and I don't have the cash so the sale is postponed until I come to the fair again at the end of the trip.

There was my favorite – the thick Brazilian chicken stew-soup and then a bus ride to Copacabana where I saw for the first time "The Hunt for Red October" with Sean Connery and a young Alec Baldwin, yet today one of my favorite movies (I've read the book half a dozen times). After a return to the modest hotel I packed my bags for Salvador. It turns out the hotel room phone calls are expensive for my modest budget: $17 USD.

The news from the phone calls: my book on Cuíca de Santo Amaro at the Jorge Amado Foundation in Salvador is indeed in process, but Carlos Cunha had no specifics other than that it will be part of an important collection at the Foundation and will incidentally have my picture on the back cover. Most important will be the preface by Jorge Amado himself! I wrote, "I think this will actually happen!"

"Keah, I really liked your Father's Day Card to me and I hope Mother's Day turned out well for you and Katie."

Departure from Rio and the flight to Salvador

Taking an early taxi to the airport was a good plan; it turned out to take a long time to arrange my "Air Pass" for this trip. It was a turbulent flight, lots of bouncing up and down. Most interesting were the Brazilian fellows seated to my right in the row: they go to the interior of Bahia State, buy used cars at a cheap price and sell them for a high price in Rio. The Brazilian version of the used car salesmen in the U.S. and both have much in common.

Now in Salvador in the airport, I caught the "frescão" to the Barra Turismo Hotel and then made phone calls to Carlos Cunha and Edilene Matos and then to friend Mário Barros in Itapuã. Cunha is on a roll and is speaking enthusiastically of the book on Cuíca de Santo Amaro. There is time for a much needed nap amidst heavy tropical rain in the city.

A Curious Aside: I met "Miss Black Illinois" from Chicago on the flight to Salvador; she is involved with a Varig promotion to encourage tourism from that huge city to Brazil and Salvador. I can only imagine her reaction to the ups and downs of Brazilian life and to those "mulatas" in Salvador (she was not really familiar with Brazilian culture or Portuguese) and also to the racial prejudice even in this the most "African" of Brazilian cities.

The "Pelourinho" and the "Fundação Casa de Jorge Amado"

The remodeled "Pelourinho," Salvador, 1990

Mark, the Exu T-Shirt, the "Fundação Casa de Jorge Amado," Salvador

Book covers from the Amado exposition and Curran's Book on Jorge Amado

The "Our Lady of the Rosary" ["Nossa Senhora do Rosário"] Church in the Pelourinho

I went to the Jorge Amado Foundation and had a nice conversation with Cláudio in charge of publications. The proofs of the book are not ready due to a computer problem, so there will be no publishing or autograph party during this stay in Brazil. It is the first day after two months' absence back at work for the Foundation's director Myriam Fraga; her husband suffered a heart attack, there was a stop of the flow of oxygen to the brain, thus a need for surgery and he almost lost control of the nervous system. I sympathized as best I could.

Preliminaries - My book "Cuíca de Santo Amaro – Poeta Repórter da Bahia" at the Jorge Amado Foundation

The Foundation wants personal information for the fly leaf of the book; they already have the photo. The book is the 5th in the series and I will be in good company; it is projected to be approximately 140 pages. I am the first to pay only a partial subsidy; all the others paid the full amount or cost of publication. The two thousand dollars represents one-third of the cost. The dedication will be to my brother Jim – "Thank you once again!" Cunha already has a note in the papers: "The book is arriving!" A beautiful publishing party ["lançamento"] is being planned, perhaps for November. The book will be controversial, but Jorge Amado wants it. It is important locally that a "Brazilianist" from the U.S. is interested in the theme, but the negative side of Cuíca de Santo Amaro will enter into debate. Cunha says, "Prepare to defend yourself."

Reencounter with Carlos, Edilene and the family

Bruno, Carlos, Carol and Edilene at Home

I had lunch with Carlos, Edilene and the kids at home. One should recall that they "saved the day" for me socially in Bahia over the years. It is incredible to see what they have to do to earn a living. Carlos is at the "Academia de Letras da Bahia" as Executive Director and at the "Instituto Joaquim Nabuco." Edilene is in charge of the Literature Section at the Cultural Foundation of the State of Bahia and is lecturing full time at the Catholic University of Bahia, five classes, four nights a week.

Carol and Bruno are 14 and 13 respectively; he is starting the guitar; both are in English classes. Gaia is the new Dalmatian puppy.

Potpourri of Bahia

I am taking three to four showers a day in Bahia; the humidity is killing me and I'm not as young or accustomed to the climate as back in the 1960s. The Bahia that I knew, the "old upper and lower city" is now poorer and of more humble class. The middle and upper classes are now on the "orla" or seaside outside of the old city. The streets in the old city seem like an Egyptian Bazaar.

I received a phone call from Neuma Borges in João Pessoa; Átila de Almeida will welcome me to see the "cordel" collection, so I'm going to João Pessoa on the 17th arriving at midnight. Neuma's husband Zé Elias will pick me up at the airport. The plan is to take the bus the next day the 18th to Campina Grande. We'll see. I'm very hopeful.

There also was a call from old Arizona days friend Mário Barros. His company Formac was robbed this afternoon by five men armed with shotguns and some of the employees were beaten up. Fortunately no one was wounded by bullets or killed. Thanks be to God. Mário thinks the thieves were former employees. I'll find out more when we have lunch tomorrow.

I had dinner that day with Carlos and Edilene and was able to play some classic guitar for them.

Here is the national economic and political news: each day there is gradually more news via the TV on the economic plan-package ["o pacote"] by the Collor de Mello government, the infamous "Plano Cruzélia" which will be scandal ridden; it's all very complicated. Collor's Minister of Finance, Cruzélia is mixed up in a love affair with a federal judge. I said to myself: "I need to get my work done and get out of here. All hell is going to break loose in Brazil; there is going to be some kind of social explosion or the like. The country has never seen anything like it." I'll buy a "Veja" magazine tomorrow and try to get caught up on all the details.

What is the average citizen to do? Carlos Cunha keeps their funds (in very modest quantities) in several banks, taking the minimum out of each one just to keep up with daily expenses. It is frightening. All bank accounts are now frozen by the government!

The cultural foundations have not paid their employees for fifteen days, and in fact the government has plans to close all the foundations including even FUNARTE,

EMBRA-FILME and I think even the Rui Barbosa Foundation in Rio. I will learn much more when Mário Barros and I meet soon.

An Aside on "Cordel:" the researcher Josepy Luyten has a very expensive book on "cordel" in Japan, in Japanese language of course.

An Aside on the research on Cuíca de Santo Amaro: Carlos Cunha tells me that Jorge Amado did his first interview with Cuíca for the magazine "Diretrizes" in 1943 using the pen name of "João Garcia." This interview would be the basis for Amado's famous pages on Cuíca in his guidebook "Bahia de Todos os Santos" with continuous printings and editions over the years since the 1940s. (I wrote in my first travel-adventure book on Brazil that I purchased said guide book and tried to see everything Amado wrote about, this in my introduction to Salvador in 1966.)

An Aside on my book on Cúica de Santo Amaro: the Bahian Journalist Paulo Marconi has done a lot of research and interviews on Cuíca and has a "dossier" on the poet's supposedly "criminal" activities. He says it represents ten years of work; he may or may not publish it.

It is during this stay in Bahia that I purchased the classic and now rare book of black and white photography of Bahia by Pierre Verger that includes rare photos of both Cuíca de Santo Amaro and Rodolfo Coelho Cavalcante selling "cordel" in the streets and at the Mercado Modelo in the 1940s!

Carlos Cunha's "silver tongue" says that my book will maintain the popular image of Cuica. Jorge Amado wants the book because it will create more interest in his own books and characters. It is good for the Foundation because of my subsidy, no matter how modest. And the fact the book was done by a "Brazilianist" does no harm. It will go out of print quickly. The old generation in Bahia (the intellectuals, the politicians) will be interested and will enter into the debate and the polemic.

Morning breakfast: we had "cuscus" - the same dish as on the sternwheeler on the São Francisco in 1967 – and "suco de cajú."

Later that day I enjoyed the last meal at "A Portuguesa" because the restaurant disappeared later.

Dona Carmina, Dom Amândio, the "Portuguesa" restaurant

Dona Miquelina hard at work in the kitchen of "A Portuguesa"

The author at the "Fundação Casa de Jorge Amado"

I took a "frescão" to the Praça da Sé and walked to the Foundation. There was a big hurry to take the publicity photos for the book. The nervous photographer first forgot to take the cap off his lens and then forgot to use the flash. It was taking a long time and I was sweating like crazy because we are on the fourth or fifth floor of the Foundation with the window view out to the Pelourinho and no air conditioning. See the photo; it was worth it.

Back to the hotel where I took shower number two of the day. Later there would be lunch with Mário Barros in the "Yate Club da Bahia," with "casquinha de sirí, paté de peixe, cenouras, azeitonas, duas batidas ótimas de limão, salada de maionese, camarão ao alho, pastel de chocolate e café." Puxa! ("Wow"). The conversation was long and great.

The News: Laís is working at the kids' school. Carlos has applied for "American Field Service," but not necessarily in the U.S. It could be Australia or in Europe.

The greater part of the conversation was over the state of the Brazilian economy, a matter so complicated that it was almost impossible for me to understand. Mário says business at the firm is actually better because the Brazilian government is "squeezing the people" and is using their money.

An Aside: when Mário says he is "going to the city," these days that means Pituba with the Civic Center, etc.! The old Bahia I knew no longer is "the place," at least for business.

Mário says that any savings they have in order to be protected are placed in the "overnight." With the new government economic plan "Cruzélia – Collor" the government now controls 80 per cent of this money. Mário considers it lost for good.

He adds that it is a way of life: all Brazilians and all the companies do their utmost to avoid paying taxes, but he thinks now with the Collor Plan that there will be a return to more honesty. Wealthy Brazilians guard their savings in gold or dollars and never in "cruzados."

Another aspect of the "Cruzélia" package: citizens can pay bills with the frozen "cruzados" in the banks, that is, the taxes owed to the government, but that's all. And this only applies until March 15, 1990. It is not permitted to write personal checks from bank accounts with "cruzados." I do not understand all this but I do understand that there is a terrible crazy rush to avoid personal disaster. Mário is sure there will be considerable unemployment; I think there will be social unrest. All the doctors are on strike and the buses will be on strike the 21st of the month.

As Aside to the Economic Disaster: There was a tremendous view from the "Yate Club" out onto the Bay of Bahia. With the atmosphere, the food and all, this was one of the moments (and they were extremely rare for me) when I witnessed the "other Brazil" once in a while over the years. It was quite a change from the markets and the world of "cordel," right?

Tourism in Salvador, 1990

Façade of the "Igreja da Terceira Ordem" of St. Francis, Salvador

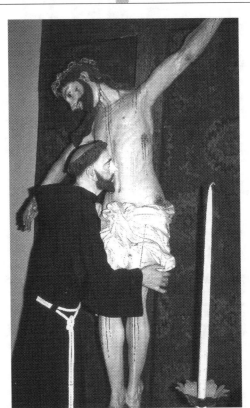

St. Francis contemplating the wounds of Christ

The bay from the Lacerda Elevador

I took a bus to the "Igreja da Terceira Ordem" and to the "Igreja de São Francisco" to its side and got some good photos later of the Bay of Bahia and the Modelo Market. Later I bought some tourist t-shirts, had lunch at "The Portuguesa" and later saw Carlos, Edilene and the family and took more photos.

That p.m. there was a swim at Barra Beach and then Mário Barros picked me up for dinner at their home with fine food and fun conversation in an extremely pleasant meeting.

Salvador to João Pessoa

The plane was on time but we had to wait an hour in Recife for connecting passengers from São Paulo and arrived in João Pessoa at one in the morning. I was lodged in what they call an "Apart-Hotel" which was rather expensive and in passing had lousy lighting for my writing.

Encounter with Átila de Almeida, consulting his "cordel" arquive

I caught an inter-urban bus in Brazil once again feeling nostalgic ["matando saudades"] for the old research days in the 1960s. It was a two hour trip from João Pessoa to Campina Grande with interesting scenery; I swear that nothing in the countryside had changed in twenty-five years! I was lodged in a very modest hotel in the old downtown with roaring music coming from the Plaza.

I went to Átila's house right away on a narrow street climbing up the hill from the plaza. We must have talked for two hours; he showed me the collection ever so briefly and turned to other topics. He is as they say in Brazil "um grande prosista," ["a good conversationalist"]. I got 95 per cent of what he said, fortunately, and the conversation was sprinkled with anecdotes and a lot of funny stories and comments. He by the way at this time is a retired Mathematics Professor!

The "cordel" collection is quite old; it comes from his father who collected in the "heyday" of old "cordel" and Átila continued the effort. He once again showed me the collection, vast as it is in long rows of many shelves, and allowed me to select some twenty story-poems, take them to the hotel and make hand written notes. He promised to Xerox them later and mail the copies to me in Rio at the Casa de Rui Barbosa (he did fulfill the promise). I spent that entire night until the wee hours reading and taking notes and was rewarded with a tremendous headache for my troubles. In the end I owe much to Neuma and Zé Elias for arranging all this. Átila did show great trust allowing me to take the poems to the hotel (there are famous accounts in the annals of "cordel" of story-poems and even of entire collections disappearing). I earned and kept his trust by faithfully returning all the "folhetos" to him at his house the next a.m.

I forgot to say that I had spent the entire day before perusing the catalogue of 13,000 poems making bibliographical entries on note cards. The conversation at lunch was fun as well; I had brought a nice gift from Arizona, a Navajo Sand Painting and a good book on Navajo Culture which were unusual for them and much appreciated.

The return to João Pessoa

After saying goodbye to Átila and his wife I returned to the hotel, checked out and caught the return bus to João Pessoa. An Aside: Átila was suffering from cancer at this time and died shortly thereafter; I never had another chance to be with him. A curious aside: I recall that when I arrived at his house the first time he was just coming home from the market with one of those huge jugs of Brazilian sugar cane rum ["cachaça"], an understandable purchase under the circumstances. It would not be until 2005 at the new library of the University of Paraíba II in Campina Grande that I would quickly view the old collection now donated and made part of that library. This latter visit was not for research but much more of a nostalgic memory of it all.

Zé Elias and Neuma picked me up at the bus station in João Pessoa and we went immediately to the beach for icy cold beer and shrimp, a wonderful lunch. Later there was a long drive to the airport where the airline put me on a waiting list (there was overbooking) and we had to return "home" with Neuma and Zé Elias. For me it was a fortunate delay because we had long conversations and I really got to know them better. There was of course much talk of "cordel" and the goings on of the University of Paraíba, but other things too. Zé Elias is a specialist in Linguistics, in the indigenous languages of the "Cariri" Region and their history, but he is also a civil engineer! Their home appears to be middle class and is in a nice part of town, the beach community of Manaíra. One son Eduardo is doing engineering at the University of Paraíba, another, Guilherme, is doing the famous university entrance exam ["vestibular," a Brazilian Institution].

My Portuguese is just so-so, good for a "gringo," but still with many errors. Neuma showed me many books on "cordel" from Portugal and Spain and Xerox copies of the "classics" from Câmara Cascudo's "Cinco Livros do Povo." Enough! I am exhausted!

So we tried another run to the airport and there was a long wait (evidently this is normal in João Pessoa), but it all finally worked out. I owe them so much, fine people of great hospitality, good intellectuals and special treatment for this "cordel" researcher from abroad.

The plane arrived in Recife where I tried to make reservations for the rest of the trip and the return flight to Rio. Then there was a small problem: they put me on a waiting list again (this was common in those days with the "Air Pass," due primarily to the cuts forced by the "Plano Collor" already discussed). My "Air Pass" is about to expire so I made an "executive decision," a bit on the impulsive side but good: it was the last time to see something new in Brazil, so I was ticketed for Iguaçu and the Falls but without a hotel reservation. I was also tired from the time in João Pessoa and Campina Grande with the heat, the noise of TV in the hotel and a general lack of sleep.

Suddenly, the trip to Iguaçu Falls and the dam at Itaipu

Everything happened extremely quickly. They took me off the flight from Recife to Rio and on to another in order to make connections with Rio – São Paulo – Iguaçu. The flight from Recife was in a DC Airbus, very luxurious; I deserved it, tired and exhausted.

South Zone, Rio de Janeiro

The skyscrapers and pollution of São Paulo

The rural zone, State of Paraná

The flight was almost empty to São Paulo so I could go to a window on the right hand side of the airplane with an incredible view of Rio, its beach and the coast; I got some excellent slides on the occasion. With just a short sleeved shirt from hot, tropical João

Pessoa, I almost froze to death in the air conditioning. Later in Iguaçú I would encounter cold and wind and was only saved by the generosity of a fellow tourist who loaned me a heavy woolen sweater. Speaking of the cold, the man at the reception desk of the modest lodging in Foz de Iguaçú wore a huge woolen topcoat. All this was something new for the gringo accustomed to the tropical heat of Brazil.

All the hotels in Iguaçu were full but I found an unranked (no stars) boarding house – Patt's – for, can you believe it, $7.50 USD. It had a dormitory with two regular beds and four bunk beds but with a shower with extremely hot water and heavy down covers on the bed. I went to bed with my teeth chattering – a first in Brazil – and with three blankets on top of me. I slept the best that night on this trip to Brazil. Amen.

There was a great breakfast the following morning. "They eat like pigs here in the South!" There was hot pizza, slices of pineapple and pineapple juice, several different types of cheese, good French bread with marmalade and "café com leite," all included in that ridiculous price already mentioned.

The next day that Japanese-Brazilian tourist lent me the sweater; I noted he was reading a comic book of "Batman" in Portuguese. Everybody was with a warm coat or overcoat; it was 4 degrees Celsius, 40 degrees Fahrenheit.

Itaipú Dam and the Lake

Mark in front of the dam at Itaipu

I waited forty minutes for a bus to Itaipu Dam, at that time the largest in the world. At eight kilometers wide, it was also the widest in the world. All we tourists saw the film at the visitor center showing its construction. We were driven in a Kombi (Volkswagen Bus) on the top of the dam and saw the huge turbines and the water rushing from the concrete tunnels of the spillway. It was an amazing sight. I spent some of the time recalling my brother Jim who worked in the management of large construction projects all over the United States.

Then I caught the bus to the town of Foz de Iguaçu, an incredible place with people from three countries – Brazil, Argentina and Paraguay. I saw no black people but there were some "mestiços." The poor here are white, quite a change from the Northeast, Recife, Salvador or even Rio de Janeiro. I thought: What if I would have pursued the research project suggested by friend Mário Barros originally from Porto Alegre and worked on Luís Fernando Veríssimo in Rio Grande do Sul State? What a difference!

The "Hotel das Cataratas" and the pool

"I have a new place to bring you Keah!" I took a bus to the falls. The famous hotel looks very nice from the outside but on the inside is really showing the wear and tear of its years. The gardens are pretty as is the pool; the tariff for this 4-Star Hotel is $75 USD (with a 15 per cent discount with the Varig Air Pass). There was a splurge for me – the noon buffet in the hotel: "maionese, ros bife mal passado, tomates, galinha, puré de batata com molho de carne ["gravy" like at home], the latter for the first time in Brazil. Icy beer to wash it down. And dessert – real lemon merengue pie! The bill was $11 USD and worth every penny! (I am writing these notes sitting on the bed of my little "pensão" with all the covers on, the borrowed sweater and my hat on my head!)

Gallery of photos of the falls

Mark and the first view of the falls

Coati Mundi on the trail at Iguaçu

"The Devil's Mouth" ["Boca do Diabo"] Iguaçu

The falls at water level

The falls and the view of Argentina across the way

Above the falls at water's edge

It was one of the most beautiful scenes in my life: the falls seemed to go on without end, better than I even had imagined. If so desired one can take a helicopter ride above it all. The view from the tower of the hotel was good, but not from the rooms (I cajoled one of the maids to let me check this out). It is impressive: one gets off the bus and boom!

The splendor of the falls is right in front of you. There is a good trail all along; I saw many coati mundi and beautiful, different butterflies. Each time one turns in a bend in the trail there is an entirely new and amazing view. The wooden walkway at the foot of one of the falls was closed during my visit, a pity, "But Keah, one day we will be here together." The hotel was not that good an experience this time around because of the dozens of Argentine and French tourists (few North Americans were visible). I read the latest paper in the lobby and was surprised to see that Phoenix beat the Los Angeles Lakers, a miracle!

The other side of the falls is Argentina and one could see the tourists in the distance (I surmise they were staring at us as well). It was here that they filmed "The Mission" with Jeremy Irons and Robert de Niro, a "classic" I showed and recommend to anyone really interested in the Jesuit missionary experience with the natives of southern Brazil and Paraguay, notwithstanding the Hollywood "take" on it all. The role of the falls was not a small one.

So it was that without a tour agency package, I paid $7.50 for a really comfortable room and breakfast, 15-25 cents for the bus ride, round trip. Such a deal.

Upon returning to the little boarding house there was beer, national news on the "TV Repórter" in Portuguese, a hot shower and to bed. "The plane leaves at 1 p.m. tomorrow but first I'm going to take a deep breath and take the local bus to Paraguay! They say it is mainly casinos and contraband and there is little crime; this tourist is not so sure about that." "Keah, I thought a lot about you today; I want to bring you here, stay at the "Hotel das Cataratas" and take all this in."

A funny aside: I just recalled that in Paraiba all the husbands seem to shout orders at their wives. Machismo has not disappeared in Brazil's Northeast (Franklin Machado's "cordel" poem "Debate of Lampião with an American Tourist" proves my point).

What else can you expect? The brand name on the billboards for beer is "Kaiser," and one sees names like "Bosch." On the Paraguay side there is much new construction of tall buildings, condos one surmises. It is the capital of all smuggling ["moamba"] in all of Latin America. The Brazilians come, fill their bags with the "moamba," all this on the Paraguay side which is a "free port," mainly with electronics. And home! I can never forget and highly recommend to the curious reader Luís Fernando Veríssimo's short story "The Lambreta." It is a small jewel.

Notes on Paraná State and Iguaçu

It was surprising to see men in winter clothing, men that looked more like U.S. citizens; it was another country down here! The waiters and waitresses in the restaurants were white. The Portuguese accent here in Paraná and Curitiba has the final R pronounced like English – Falarrrr!

The next morning I took a deep breath and climbed on the jammed bus from Foz to Paraguay; we crossed the International Bridge high above the Paraguay River. It is a free zone, like Nogales, Arizona – Mexico but very congested. The streets were jammed with contraband items ["moamba"]: watches, electronic devices and a surprise – fishing rods and reels from Japan of high quality. I looked at some samples of Paraguayan folk art but was not moved to purchase any. The Brazilians, on the other hand, would drive their cars for days to arrive at this scene, fill the huge luggage bags with "stuff" including TV sets. Everything was cheaper than in Brazil, but there was a certain uncleanliness surround the entire market scene.

Now on the other side in Foz in Brazil, I left the boarding house - hotel early and took a taxi to the airport. It was a very good decision to come here but if Keah and I come it will have to be first class at the "Hotel das Cataratas."

The return to Rio de Janeiro - Potpourri of Rio

I slept just so-so and then took a bus to the Rui Barbosa Foundation to Xerox more story-poems; the subway has been on strike this entire trip. My stomach is in an uproar so that is not good. I spoke with Adriano da Gama Kury at the Casa; things are so bad that employees are bringing their own toilet paper!

Homero Senna wants me to pay to publish "Grande Sertão: Veredas e a Literatura de Cordel" or take it out of José Olympio Publishing House.

I went to the National Institute of Folklore (in an annex of the fantastic old presidential palace, "O Palácio do Catete,") perused the collection list of some 2,500 story-poems and Xeroxed about a dozen for the future book "História do Brasil em Cordel."

Tomorrow it's the National Library and FUNARTE, the National Foundation of the Arts.

On yet another day after a bus to the city (downtown) I had to deal with the bureaucracy of the National Library: the "cordel" collection was actually housed in the old Ministry of Education Building which housed the National Institute of Folklore in my very first days of research in Rio de Janeiro in 1966-1967. This was where I was introduced to Renato Almeida and later good friend Vicente Salles (director of the "Revista Nacional de Folclore" and later "Cultura" magazine in Brasília). I saw only three "folhetos" that I wanted and called it a day.

I decided at that time that I would not travel alone to Brazil to do more research; it was just too lonely. Perhaps to a conference with others I knew.

There was one surprise: a prize winning book published in 1985 and housed in the National Library cited many of the books of the "grande estudioso" Mark J. Curran: the Pernambuco book from 1973, several scholarly articles and the book on Jorge Amado from 1980. It was still grating on my nerves that the Federal University of Pernambuco had not published the revised and augmented version of "A Literatura de Cordel" of 1973, reneging on promises to do so. (I remedied this at Trafford Publishing in the U.S. years later.)

I just spoke on the telephone to Manuel Diégues Júnior who wrote the best study on "cordel" for the volume of studies at the Casa de Rui Barbosa in 1973. The owner of a fine collection of "cordel," along with Manuel Cavalcanti Proença and Orígenes Lessa in those days, Manuel said to me: "The collection is gone; there is no more; I distributed it." This was yet another of the fateful stories over the years of what happened to good and important "cordel" collections; and it provided food for thought as to my own in future years.

I telephoned Keah at ten p.m. that night; it was a bad connection, but everything was all right. I was relieved.

Luís Raimundo Fernandes and Mark at the country place

There was a reunion with good friend Luís Raimundo whom I met at the boarding house years earlier in Salvador. It turned into a bit of an adventure. We went first to a car repair shop on the outskirts of Rio and later to the farm at Santa Cruz via "Avenida Brasil," the road that goes from Rio along the coast to Santos, the major port of São Paulo State. The country place was indeed pretty with a nice house, swimming pool, beautiful gardens and fruit trees. The highlight of the day was the TV and the Formula I races which are important in Brazil (many famous drivers including Emerson Fittipaldi and especially Ayrton Senna). However, the drive home was tense since the car was practically without brakes and had a dragging tail pipe which I was sure was going to cause a fire. Luís Raimundo on the other hand was not worried at all.

On yet another day I returned to the Hippy Fair in Ipanema to buy that leather image of the Portuguese Caravel (the "Antocha") I had seen at the beginning of the trip. Alas and bad luck for me, it had been sold in the interim when I was up north for research. I did buy a beautiful version of another Tall Ship, the "Cutty Sark," but it was not the same. On the other hand, I purchased Glauco's "Mapa Mundi" with perhaps three small caravels interspersed throughout the planet, a treasure and good memory for me yet today. It hangs above my writing desk in the cabin in Colorado and provides great inspiration for the tasks.

A new cold started yesterday, that plus continuing stomach problems. Ai!

I finally went to José Olympio and took out my study of João Guimarães Rosa's "Grande Sertão: Veredas" and the "Literatura de Cordel" (the one that garnered me the prize in 1985 and that great trip to Brazil with Keah). The good news was that it was totally prepared for publication and with my Portuguese corrected. The bad news: the odyssey for its publication would continue but all would turn out extremely well; it came out as the feature article in "Brazil/ Brasil" a major publication at Brown University in 1994. An Aside: With the economic crisis affecting all Brazil these days the old, venerable José Olympio Editora, one of the most famous traditional publishing houses in Brazil, was upon hard times; it was only publishing new editions of older books.

At the Casa de Rui yesterday I received the Xeroxes of the story-poems from Campina Grande from Átila de Almeida, promise fulfilled! And thank you Átila! At this point in 1990 I had sufficient material for a good new book in the future (it would become the book from the University of São Paulo Press in 1998).

Mark, Cristina and Henrique Kerti

I ate dinner with Cristina and Henrique that night, not knowing it would be the last time before Henrique's death. It was at this point the trip ended.

I would return to Brazil one more time in 1990 this time to old Salvador for the publication and autograph party for the book on Cuíca de Santo Amaro. The story is in the next chapter of "Diary III."

CHAPTER IV

NOVEMBER OF 1990. TRIP TO SALVADOR DA BAHIA, BRAZIL

Motive: Publication of "Cuíca de Santo Amaro – Poeta Repórter da Bahia" at the "Fundação Casa de Jorge Amado" in Salvador

The arrival in Salvador, moments and encounters before the book autograph party

Mark in the upper window of the Jorge Amado Foundation, the "Pelourinho" in the background

casa de
PALAVRAS

´mark j. curran

cuíca
de santo amaro
poeta - repórter
da bahia

Fundação Casa de Jorge Amado

Curran's book published at the Jorge Amado Foundation

Arriving at the hotel in Bahia I phoned Carlos Cunha; the book is ready and the autograph party will be Thursday evening at the Foundation with a small seminar, all sponsored by Myriam Fraga the director of the Foundation. Three or four local experts on Cuíca will participate; there will be cocktails, "acarajé," and "cordel" poets reciting verse. Cunha is enthusiastic; it could be his good ole' flattery and silver tongue but he says, "Imagine! An American with three books on Bahian culture!"

They gave me a copy of the invitation to the "Lançamento" as proof to ASU for my expenses on the trip. Cunha says they invited people from USIS (United States Information Service), IBEU (Brazilian-United States Institute), the large English language school in Salvador, and 500 Bahians. There will be an exposition of all the books by Jorge Amado and the publications of the Foundation. I hope Katie's camera works well (borrowed for just this trip). There are already notes in the local papers and a life-size cardboard mockup of Cuíca by the artist Sinésio Alves. Dona Maria de Carmo, Cuíca's widow will be present and will receive a stipend from the Foundation. Myriam's husband is recuperating from the heart attack and is doing better. So goes Cunha's news on the phone. He adds that Jorge Amado is in France and I should be sure and send a copy of the book to him.

I called Mário Barros and left a message for him with Carla the daughter; Laís is in Porto Alegre attending to her ill mother.

Sketch-Caricature of the poet Cuíca de Santo Amaro

On another day I was with Myriam at the Foundation. I saw the programs and THE BOOK! After all this time it was a moment of great accomplishment and happiness, and it was good looking. There were newspaper articles in the three major dailies of Salvador, all with long articles on Cuíca, the book and a photo of yours truly. Mário Barros called and said, "You are famous in Bahia."

I am suffering from stress and not sleeping well; this will all change after the event. The book exposition has been done ahead of time, is well done, and is located in the principal salon after you enter from the "Pelourinho." Notes on the book were sent to all parts of Brazil.

There was a special lunch at Carlos and Edilene's house: it was Bruno's birthday: chicken, shrimp and ice cream of course! I had brought presents for Edilene: the Navajo Plates and Sand Paintings from Arizona. It turns out she did no less than four revisions of the book, checking my Portuguese. It was worth it; it reads well. Cunha did all the publicity. Theirs is my "second home" away from Arizona in Bahia.

The new Pelourinho and the Jorge Amado Foundation

Professionally speaking, the book is a good thing for me (and for ASU). It incidentally gains in prestige with Jorge Amado's fine preface.

Life here is difficult, more expensive as time goes by. Edilene is lecturing at the Catholic University. The Cultural Foundation of the State of Bahia is a disaster; there is no funding. The Jorge Amado Foundation is a bit better off but still with difficulties. The city seems to be one fair or market, like am Egyptian or Turkish bazaar in the streets.

I offered to give a short lecture to Edilene's literature class at the "Católica." The building and its classrooms were in lamentable shape compared to our U.S. prosperity at ASU. I did comment on this to Edilene and she was struck by the impression on a foreigner (I guess they are used to it in Salvador). I wrote, "We are lucky to be living in the U.S."

Carlos and Edilene are happy with the book and the autograph party; it is a good moment for them and for the Foundation. I am a bit preoccupied by the negative side of Cuíca de Santo Amaro and how that will come out in the debate. Cunha says not to worry; he is confident I can defend myself and my thesis. TV reporters will be present. I wish you were here Keah! Mário phoned; he will try to be present at the event. Laís is still in Porto Alegre with her mother. Perhaps we can meet later.

Back at the Foundation I spent time seeing all the newspaper clippings so far concerning the event and the publicity. There was a long talk with Cláudio the head of publishing for the Foundation. He said they would mail my share of the books (due to the subvention); I took a packet of fifty of them with me to the hotel, a good thing because the promised books never arrived! "I'm tired by now, back at the hotel, trying to rest; the event is late this afternoon."

Curran in Front of the Jorge Amado Foundation in Salvador

The book autograph party

It did not come up to the beauty and magnificence of the "50 Years of Literature of Jorge Amado" commemoration back in 1981 (as could be expected), but it was good. I arrived early, this in spite of the taxi that broke down in the middle of Avenida 7 on the way to the "Pelourinho." The taxi driver was a "man of the people," and I probably understood 20 per cent of what he said. I was dressed in good clothes for the presentation and found myself sweating like a pig there in the middle of the street waiting to see what the driver could do. You had to see it! I do not recall but think I flagged another taxi or bus, and arrived at the "Terreiro de Jesus," near the "Pelourinho." There was time for a short prayer in São Francisco Church (where better?) and time to wander around the tourist shops in the Pelourinho.

At the Foundation I was invited to join Myriam Fraga in her upper floor office joining Hildegardes Viana (from 1966 days) and Junot Silveira, a reporter with fifty years of service for "A Tarde" and with many encounters and recollections of Cuíca de Santo Amaro. On the ground floor and the main salon the public was arriving and TV Bahia ("Rede Globo") was filming. I was introduced to many local persons but in the stress of it all remember few names.

There was a TV interview but it was shown that night at 10 p.m. and I never got a chance to see it, but think it turned out well. I talked of the importance of Cuíca, why I did the book, "cordel," Jorge Amado, his novels and relationship to Cuíca.

It was time for the talks. Sinésio Alves compared Cuíca to a "Brazilian Charlie Chaplin."

Edilene Matos spoke of the first interview with Cuíca by Jorge Amado in 1943. Junot Silveira spoke on I know not what. Myriam Fraga followed with some anecdotes about the poet. Then the poet Maria Preta recited some poetry. The culmination of all this was the iconoclast poet of "cordel" Lucena de Mossoró (an occasional poem of his appears in my books, most notably the pseudo journalistic account of the bomb at Guararapes Airport in Recife in 1966 when "guerrillas" tried to kill upcoming military president Costa e Silva and failed). In this case Mossoró included a lot of nonsense and improvisation about many persons present. He spoke a long time and often in an offensive tone. Hildegardes followed with her memories of the poet.

I made a point of speaking privately with Dona Maria do Carmo, Cuíca's widow (she received 11.000 "cruzeiros" from the Jorge Amado Foundation, $110 USD. It amounts to two months of minimum wage salary in Brazil.) I told her that I had treated Cuíca well and placed him in a national perspective. I recalled that I was with her at her modest house in Liberdade years back when I was actually doing the fieldwork research for the future book, an interview arranged by Carlos Cunha.

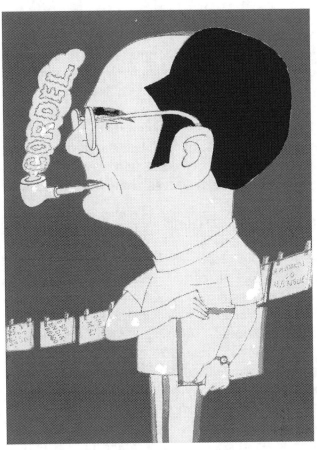

Sketch-Caricature of Curran by Sinésio Alves

I signed books for about an hour. See the photo of the cardboard mockup of Cuíca by Sinésio Alves. He spoke privately with me and told an anecdote: he and his wife were in their car parked in front of their house. Thieves with shotguns came, robbed the car and later destroyed it. Sinésio told all of this with much humor indicating perhaps his terrific attitude toward life and its vicissitudes.

A light bulb just went off in my brain: my next book should be about Sinésio with interviews from him and his illustrations. He is genuinely a good person; as they say, "a heart of gold." (Recall Machado de Assis's description in one of his satiric novels: "He is a heart of gold with gold.") Sincere. Humble. I never got around to doing the book and Sinésio died a few years back. Sad. It would have been one of those truly pleasurable researches and the product would have pleased and entertained many people.

Sinésio's cardboard "mockup" of Cuíca de Santo Amaro which decorated the autograph party.

Mário Barros and his father set up a time for lunch; they did attend the party.

The attendance at the book party according to Carlos Cunha was quite a bit less than they had anticipated. He attributed it to the fact that the public was still afraid to come to the "Pelourinho" at night, this in spite of the fact there was police security surrounding the building that night.

Reencounter with Mário Barros

Curran and Mário Barros at Formac

I was with the Barros for the mid-day meal at the "Yate Club." My appetite was better now after the book party and the stress of that, plus the good company. The meal was "siri de caranguejo, azeitonas, queijo, batida de limão, salada de camarão, um bife grande e gostoso, farofa e fritas."

Mário Barros working at the office

I visited the firm where Mário works, "A Formac," and it was a good experience. I saw the office with all the computers; the firm has branch offices and sales offices in the interior of the State. Mário has been with the firm sixteen years in Bahia and three years prior to that in the South. I saw him working, a true professional. The principal task at present was to obtain loans from the banks so the customers could pay their debts to Formac.

Mário did an arrangement ("um jeito") with a friend at Varig and they arranged for me a flight on the 28th for Rio with a VIP check in at the Hotel da Bahia.

The last night with Carlos and Edilene

I was much more relaxed now. Edilene said in an aside that "You are indeed very persistent." She had thought that all hope for the book was lost in the time of Olívia Barradas, the then head of the Cultural Foundation of the State of Bahia. It had been Cunha's idea to write directly to Jorge Amado and, "Boom! It all happened." She spoke of Sebastião Batista, Lourival Batista and new projects: Castro Alves and "cordel," "cordel" in Bahia, and parodies in "cordel." She mentioned that Sinésio Alves had recently done the carnival decorations for the President in Brasília. An aside: Carlos and Edilene would separate in the coming years. I would not see Carlos again; in fact he avoided personal contact with me on a couple of occasions after this when I was in Bahia. I discovered later that it was not only my case; he was depressed and refused to make many personal contacts. I was with Edilene a time or two later, once at a congress in São Paulo and much later at another in João Pessoa. She moved to São Paulo, got her Ph.D. at the University of São Paulo, remarried there and has a new life. But this time in Salvador really marked an end of an era of friendship and time with them.

I left Salvador feeling good about it all; I had persevered in the matter of the book, writing to Jorge Amado and sending him a summary of the book on Cuíca de Santo Amaro. Otherwise, nothing would have happened. A small inheritance from deceased brother Jim provided the subsidy for the book. I am justifiably proud of the accomplishment. The "Bahianos" had a hard time believing that a foreigner could have done the research for that book.

Rain, flooding and a mad rush to the airport

Nothing is easy in Salvador and the following proved it once again. There was torrential rain the entire night before my departure from Salvador and all the streets were flooded. I had to leave my lodging in Barra and go to the Hotel da Bahia to get the airline ticket home. With the flooding I could not even wade across the street in front of the hotel to catch a taxi, but did succeed in hopping a city bus to the Hotel da Bahia. Even the lobby of the hotel was flooded but I managed to get to the Varig office and get the ticket printed. Mário had arranged for me not to have to pay the $100 fee for the changes in the ticket. Recalling: the departure from my hotel was at 10:00 a.m. and the plane was due to leave at 1:40 p.m. So the odyssey began: that morning there were two hundred cross streets in the city that were flooded (a report from the radio in my taxi); the radio announced that everyone was to stay at home and not try to travel save for emergencies! A guy at the Varig office said there was no way anyone could get to the airport. Notwithstanding, I was able to contact one of those crazy Bahian taxi drivers: the ride was in a broken down old car, the driver 26 hours without sleep; he lived ten kilometers from the airport and had been trying to get home. So this was a new try. His eyes were half closed from lack of sleep as we headed out on the road along the beach ("a orla"); there we ran into barricades and had to return to the city. The traffic arteries in the valley were flooded so he put the car into low and headed up the hill to Federação; we must have had to turn around at least six times. After about an hour he succeeded in getting on the parallel interior freeway with water, mud and landslides to the side. He drove like a madman but with $22 USD in cash for payment we actually got to the airport in plenty of time for the departure.

Airplane problems and business class to Chicago

Now the irony: the plane was coming from Manaus and had broken down in São Luís de Maranhão; it was later scheduled to arrive at 3:00 p.m. There was a voucher for lunch from Varig. The flight to Los Angeles was supposed to leave at 12:30 a.m. the following day. My plan in Rio was to not leave the airport, but I found myself still waiting at the airport in Salvador.

There was more delay in Salvador but the plane finally arrived and made the flight to Rio. There at the Galeão they had put me on a waiting list for the Los Angeles flight, but as a reward for all my troubles they gave me a business class ticket on a Varig flight to Chicago leaving at 12:15 a.m. It would be the only time in all my travels in Brazil that I had such an experience, business class that is. I did not turn down the offer.

I wrote these notes in English: such was the service on the flight to Chicago:

Large seat which pulls down to stretch legs

Travel kit, hot towels, nuts, drinks, shrimp-crab salad, caviar, carrot salad, steak, dessert tray and "licores"

Breakfast: "café com leite," croissant, steak, cheese, a box of chocolates

Upon arriving at customs in Chicago there was a strong breeze outside; it was November after all. There was a long walk through the terminal to the United Airlines desk and soon the departure with the skyscrapers of Chicago out the window. And then, home.

CHAPTER V

BRAZIL 1996

Motive: Reencounter with former student Roberto Froelich in Rio de Janeiro, publications, northeastern culture and a conference in São Paulo

This short stay in Brazil would be my true introduction to the metropolis of São Paulo, to the publishing house of the University of São Paulo ("A EDUSP, A Editora da Universidade de São Paulo"), to the university itself, but equally important the introduction to the Northeastern Cultural Milieu and an important cast of characters of Northeastern artists in that huge city.

It is a little ironic that it took me so many years to enter into and take part in that cultural milieu. I believe I already mentioned that I actually was not enthusiastic about going to that huge city and dealing with that reality, and frankly, I paid no attention ["não dava bola"] to what São Paulo offered in terms of my cultural interests and research. I admit now to everyone that I was wrong and I ask myself: if São Paulo is "the greatest northeastern city outside the Northeast," and if one- third of its population is from the Northeast, how can one ignore these facts? Thus one understands my apologies. It takes nothing from the Northeast itself or the Northeastern cultural presence in Rio de Janeiro, but the "cake" would have been incomplete without it.

And as I will talk about later, in terms of the publication of my research efforts, the long hours dedicated to all this over the years, it was São Paulo that rewarded me with the best results. I am grateful; thank you.

The flight

I caught Southwest Airlines to Los Angeles and there caught the bus to the International Terminal which was chock full of Asians. Among them were a soccer team from Japan and many businessmen; our flight would be a DC 10 to Rio de Janeiro.

The in-flight service on Varig: it was now "modern," that is to say, fairly lousy, not like in those good ole' days. Everything now is plastic.

The flight to Rio was long and I was exhausted upon arrival. There was a long wait in customs but ex-student Roberto sure enough was outside in the crowd awaiting arriving passengers. He had studied Spanish Literature and Latin American Civilization with me at ASU in the 1970s and had also initiated his studies in Portuguese around the same time. I always said of him: he was my most successful student of Portuguese - he went to Brazil, loved it and never came home! Roberto was and is the epitome of the free spirit!

With Roberto Froelich in Rio

Former student Roberto and the Brazilian hot water heater

Roberto practicing classic guitar

We caught the "frescão" to Copacabana and after a long, hot walk, me sweating "buckets" with my heavy luggage, we arrived at Roberto's house. There I met his roommate Paco. There was great conversation; then Roberto played some classic guitar and then fixed a home-made Italian "macarronada" for the big mid-day meal.

We then did a walk through Leme to the edge of Copacabana and over to the big rock at the end of the beach to "Fishermen's Rock" to watch all the local fishermen, many of them retirees. They were catching a fish that looked like a small barracuda to me (surely not!) What do I know?

The first night was horrible; I could not sleep due to the humidity and to the excessive noise of the side street ("a ladeira"). The upward sloping street was the way to the back of Copacabana (Roberto's house was among the last before the hill) and then the paths up to a "favela." All I heard were cars gunning their engines, rushing up the street, honking their horns and dogs barking.

On Sunday morning we caught the "Triagem" bus to the São Cristóvão Fair in Rio's North Zone where we arrived first to the "cordel" poetry stand of Expedito da Silva, an old acquaintance of mine. Later Roberto, Paco and I drank a beer at a "forró" music stand. There was a good encounter with "cordel" poet and woodcut artist Franklin Machado, our first meeting in four years. The first was at the Casa de Rui Barbosa Foundation and a night of "farra" with Franklin, Sebastião Nunes Batista and me, an unforgettable "lesson" in "cordel" and Northeastern folklore. Separated from his wife in São Paulo, Franklin left the metropolis, did some TV work in Salvador but was now head of the "Museum of Feira de Santana" in his home town in Bahia State.

Franklin caught me up on all the news on "cordel's" poets and researchers in 1996: Edilene Matos and Carlos Cunha are now separated; she is in São Paulo pursuing a Ph.D. in Literature at the University of São Paulo. Old friend and "cordel" poet Apolônio Alves dos Santos has a "cordel" stand in Campina Grande, Paraíba State. Gonçalo Ferreira da Silva is directing the "Casa de São Saruê" in Rio de Janeiro together with General Umberto Peregrino who is now 84 years old. J. Barros and others are at the "Praça da República" in São Paulo and J. Borges is still in Bezerros in Pernambuco, the master of the northeastern woodcuts. Machado says it all is at an end in Pernambuco (my view and experience later: perhaps the "cordel," but not J. Borges; he is doing better than ever).

We caught the bus to Roberto's house where we enjoyed the leftovers from Saturday and then that night went to the "Mercadinho São José" in the district of Flamengo for an unforgettable event. The entertainment was a "chorinho" quartet, excellent in all respects, accompanied by a lot of "choppe," good conversation and a beautiful evening. All the musicians were "amateurs," and had other jobs; music was a hobby for them. The "chorinho" is a popular Brazilian type of music, not familiar to me in days in the Northeast, but rather in the center-south. No less than Heitor Vila-Lobos loved them and adapted the type and rhythm to his classical compositions in the 20th century. I recall a guitar, a flute, a type of mandolin and possibly percussion. This was my first and last time to hear a "choro" concert in Brazil.

Afterwards I invited Roberto and Paco for pizza alongside Copacabana beach; we got home at midnight and I slept like a log (they say rock or "pedra" in Portuguese) until 6:30 a.m.

We went swimming at Copacabana beach that next morning; there was high tide but one could swim and body surf ["fazer jacaré" or make like an alligator in Portuguese]. It was great; it had literally been years since I had swum at that beach. The only bad news: I succeeded in getting a very painful burn on the top of my feet ["no peito do pé"].

Dona Judite preparing "Vatapá"

That same day was set for Roberto's maid to make a special meal for us in my honor (known as a fan of Bahia): "Moqueca de peixe, vatapá, quiabo" and I might add, later: Pepto Bismal! Afterwards we went to the Rui Barbosa Foundation and it is of note that it was the shortest visit I had ever made to that old, august, familiar institution of research since 1966. Ex-Director of the Philology Section Adriano Kury was gone; Homero Senna the Ex-Director of the Research Center was retired. Nothing was going on in the "cordel" sector since the days of Orígenes Lessa; it was a new era and a sad one for me.

Roberto "putting on a show" of classic guitar at the "Guitarra da Prata"
on the "Rua do Carioca" in downtown Rio de Janeiro

Roberto and I caught the "Metrô" to downtown, went to the bookstores and then to the "Guitarra da Prata" where I had bought my rosewood DiGiorgio classic guitar in December of 1966. Roberto proceeded to give a short concert of classical and "Carioca" pieces catching everyone's attention in the shop; yours truly followed with a modest selection or two. Then there were stops at Praça Tiradentes and the "Bar Luís," according to Rio "Rotarian" Roberto, the best draft beer in Rio. Back "home" I called Abigail and Zé Rubens in São Paulo; they are friends of ASU's Clarice Deal, a colleague in Portuguese, and it was through her auspices that I made contact and would lodge with them a few days during the upcoming conference at the USP. That night there was good talk; we ate the rest of the Bahian food for supper.

Robert and the now antiquated "Big Ear" ["Orelhão"], Ipanema Beach

It was the last day in Rio, sunshine in the morning so Roberto, Paco and I caught the bus to Ipanema. Note the photo: the end of an era - the last but not unimportant pay telephone booths in Rio de Janeiro before the cellular age! We walked the beach, checked out the bookstores (a pleasure of mine for 50 years in Brazil), and ended with a fine lunch at the popular local "in" spot for food and draft beer: The "Draft Beer Syndicate" ["O Sindicato do Choppe"]. Later that afternoon at Roberto's place I was introduced to and began perusing "Bureaucracy and the Latin Americanist-'Brazilianist'" a current favorite of my host's.

That night I caught a taxi to the Kerti residence, those age-old friends in Rio. There was good conversation with Cristina (recall Henrique is now deceased), daughter Leticia and her fiancée Rodrigo. Henrique's death was a main topic of conversation, happening since my last visit to Brazil. Cristina had also worked at the packing plant in Nova Friburgo and was now running the family restaurant in Barra, needless to say a "churrascaria." The next week they were going to Angra dos Réis for a short vacation; Cristina invited us "anytime," just a matter of calling ahead and setting up the dates. They liked the idea of visiting Phoenix and Colorado. Cristina said, "We Brazilians go to Aspen." A bit different crowd than our hiking and trout fishing friends at Vallecito I'm afraid.

On that last day in Rio I was awakened at 5:00 a.m. by roosters crowing outside! Roberto accompanied me to the beach at Leme where I caught the "frescão" to Galeão

International Airport. Summing it up: this was a fine visit in 1996 between former student and professor, now just "friends." We talked about Literature: American, Argentinian, and Brazilian. There was lots of classical guitar music. And lots of laughter. The lesson taught by the professor years before was well learned by the student: read literature to learn and have fun. See humor in everything. I wrote: "Roberto may be a unique case. He remembers his roots but has developed into a true intellectual full of curiosity and possessing an open mind. But he is also an eccentric."

And one must recall the "folkloric" aspect of his apartment: the defective hot water heater and the defective "vaso" or stool as well, the Brazilian way to make coffee, how to sleep in a hammock, and the view from his living room window. The bed was also "folkloric" like the one in the boarding house in Recife, the "Chácara das Rosas:" I slept on my side two successive nights due to wooden slats before the sheets.

I forgot: it was on this brief visit to Rio that I bought that unique gift for teenage daughter Katie – a bikini from one of the "chique" shops in Leblon. The salesgirls, all Cariocas, did not know the size numbers and measurements in inches from the U.S. (naturally), all accustomed to the metrics of Rio. But that turned into a real "Carioca" style show: each would come out, do a stylish pose, and say, "Is she like this, my size?" Later Katie told me it was perfect!

Airplane to São Paulo

The Varig flight to São Paulo

It was a Boeing 437, clean, good looking and all the passengers on board seemed the same: prosperous southerners. Breakfast on board was some vague fruit and a cheese and ham croissant. There was something new for this passenger, first time on Varig – instant "café com leite" – you just open the package and add heated water. Surprisingly it was not so bad.

Skyscrapers and pollution of São Paulo

My impression of Guarulhos Airport in São Paulo: it was clean and efficient. Abigail graciously picked me up at the airport and like good "paulistanos" we took the freeway to the city. I recall mainly the potholes in the asphalt, the big trucks with diesel fumes through the industrial district, the "beltway," downtown, and the tunnels on the way to the University of São Paulo.

Arrival at the home of Abigail and Zé Rubens

Retired Varig Airlines Captain Zé Rubens and my hostess Abigail, São Paulo

I met Renato their eighteen year old son; he is studying Literature at the USP but wants to eventually do Law. Luís Paulo who is four or five is in pre-school at the university. Zé Rubens and his friend Carlos have a small business: they do export-import of articles mainly from Miami. The merchandise includes hats and sunglasses; they send all this to the towns in the São Paulo State interior. I felt comfortable at their home. A bit later Abigail had to go to the university so we had a fine mid-day lunch at the faculty club: there was a long table full of salads, including avocado, "linguiça, picanha, batata frita, arroz e café." I refrained from an icy cold draft beer because there was a meeting scheduled that p.m. at the USP Press. I commented: "The cafeteria food at ASU does not even come close!"

A great moment at the University of São Paulo Press

We arrived at the offices of the press and it was an important moment for me. Heitor Ferraz is now the "assessor" or assistant to the President of the Press Sérgio Miceli who has a new book that came out today. He is downtown now doing an interview that will come out in "Veja" Magazine.

Heitor had in his hands the complete manuscript of what would be "História do Brasil em Cordel" (the large cardboard box with the manuscript plus the diskette that I had sent through the mail). It seems that anything to do with the book had been decided, that all was indeed done. "It's a matter now of just arranging the details." They wanted me to decide on a title, send the proofs rapidly and especially the material for the illustrations ("folheto" covers, photos). It was a good thing I had brought the actual "folhetos" with me; they let me explain each one and how it would fit in the book. Speaking humbling, I think I was a good "salesman" and indeed "sold" the book to them. I believe this encounter "iced the cake" for the successful publication.

Abigail also had a chance to present her case – textbooks for clinical psychology. Everything was extremely organized and civilized; this indeed was another world apart from Pernambuco or Bahia! They called in Plínio Martins, at the time the setup man for the text and illustrations, in effect putting together the book for publishing. He seemed very enthusiastic, sharing the feelings of Heitor and Sérgio Miceli. An Aside: Plínio Martins will be the future president of EDUSP and he will be the one to publish in the future my "Retrato do Brasil em Cordel" ["Portrait of Brazil in Its Folk-Popular Poetry"] the culmination of my research work in Brazil over the years. (The text of this latter book is with the "text editor ["revisor"] in 2009; I delivered the manuscript in 2002! Something new in 2010: I just read the final proofs and the book will be out in 2011!)

Back to "História do Brasil em Cordel:" we spoke of the size of the text and the title; they want me to place some complete texts of story-poems at the end of the book and more illustrations. An Aside: There was talk of an autograph party tomorrow for a book by Jerusa Pires; perhaps I'll go.

All of a sudden Sérgio Miceli made an appearance in the room; he was extremely "simpatico," seemed genuinely friendly and happy to see me. He asked Heitor if all was in order and how was my Portuguese? "Just a joke," he says, and then "Let's get going; do it!" It was he who made the final decision on the title: "História do Brasil em Cordel." Everything happened very quickly, all saying, "Yes, yes." He did not seem worried or even particularly interested in a Volume II on recent "cordel;" "You've got to stop somewhere!" That was my sentiment as well; enough already. He said, "Come in on Monday and we will sign the contract." I believe he is speaking seriously! How different from Recife, Bahia or even Rio! They want my passport number; I will receive twenty copies and ten per cent royalty after the cost of publication (it was surprising over the years what I did receive). The initial printing will be 1,500 copies. This would be the first step in my greatest publishing success in Brazil; they would do a total of three printings in 2001 and 2003. The book would be well received in Brazil and was really the only one with significant royalties. (Writing this now in 2016 I am recalling the advice of that short story writer in Salvador – the writer of epigrams - some years ago to not mess around with Salvador and deal only with publishers in the South. He gave me this advice in 1990.)

The Institute of Brazilian Studies at the USP and other moments

I went to the USP hitching a ride with Abigail and went to the famous Institute of Brazilian Studies which "was under repairs until April." All the rows of shelves were covered with heavy plastic from ceiling to floor to protect from the construction dust. Being persistent, I did convince them to let me at least see the catalogues to their well-known "cordel" collection so highly spoken of by researchers in Brazil. I saw the lists for the Vila-Lobos Collection, as well as that of José Aderaldo Castelo, Ruth Terra, Mário de Andrade and the main catalogue of the Institute of Brazilian Studies. The surprising thing was that there were few story-poems I had not seen previously, mainly those in the first phase of Lampião. The research odyssey was over! I would go home satisfied that the important fieldwork was done.

I telephoned Mike Grossman and we set up a lunch for the next day in the "Consulado Mineiro" ["The Minas Gerais Consulate"] a nearby bar. There I met Assis Ângelo and after a few social moments, we became friends. He was the number one TV personality in all São Paulo in regard to northeastern culture.

Later I went with Abigail to the clinical psychology department at USP. She just finished her Ph.D. last year and had done the bachelor's degree in Brasília and had a practice in Rio de Janeiro (incidentally of upper class clients). But she likes teaching, has two classes and does some publishing. It is serious work; she is highly qualified in her area of research and teaching.

Waking the next day at 6:00 a.m. I hitched a ride with Abigail to the "Praça da República" in the center of São Paulo. It was early and the stands were just beginning to open – "tendas" with semi-precious stones, paintings, old coins, old stamps and what seemed to me to be "hippy" art. There seemed to be more tourist "junk" ["bugigangas"] than during my and Keah's visit to the same fair in 1985. The word is that the leather artist Glauco is now in Europe so perhaps I did not miss out on anything by not being able to go to the "Hippy" fair in Ipanema during this trip. I saw no "cordel," but there was none as well in 1985.

Encounter with the singer-poets and others at "Rádio Atual" and the Northeastern Culture Center in São Paulo

Curran and the Poets Téo Azevedo and J. Barros, São Paulo

It was through Michael Grossman and his work with the "northeastern poetic duel" ["cantoria nordestina"] in São Paulo that the events of that day happened.

The "singer-poet" ["cantador"] and our host Téo Azevedo appeared in the Praça da República at the exact agreed meeting time of 9:15 a.m. and the "cordel" poet – woodcut artist J. Barros accompanied him. J. Barros had some old story-poems that I paid $20 for just to "be social" ["quebrar o galho"].

Photo Gallery of the Center of Northeastern Culture and "Rádio Atual" and Teo de Azevedo's Radio Show

The owner of "Rádio Atual" and Father Damian in his old age

The group at "Rádio Atual"

The singer of Northeastern "Cattle Calls" ["Boiadas"] and the host Téo Azevedo

Singing "Cattle Calls" ["Boiadas"] on "Rádio Atual"

Curran and the poets, lunch at the Northeastern Cultural Center

Dancing "forró" at the Cultural Center

After meeting in the "Praça da República" we caught a taxi to a distant part of the city (there was a lot of time spent on the city freeways) and arrived at "Rádio Atual" located in one of the Northeastern Culture Centers. To one side of the main door of the radio station was a life-size statue of Father Cícero Romão, to the other the same of Friar Damian. And there were also statues of Lampião and Maria Bonita, so all the northeastern "cordel" icons were present. In front of it all was a huge plaza where all manner of cultural events were held, an example being the huge festival of St. John's Day ["Dia de São João"] the 24th of June.

Téo's program begins at 10:30 a.m.; Mike Grossman and Flávio of the "Blues Etílicos" band arrive. Téo is a true "showman" and has been doing radio for thirty years; he reminds me very much of Luís Gonzaga (of "forró" music fame) when he is "on the air." The theme of the program is Northeastern Music featuring the "sanfona" or sound box;

Téo "shoots the bull" a bit and then plays a tape or CD. All of a sudden there is the commotion of the arrival of a plethora of northeastern "singer-poets" ["cantadores"].

What I remember of the program is as follows.

Flávio of the "Blues Etílicos," a pop-rock music group extremely popular throughout Brazil at the moment, plays the "northeastern anthem," "Asa Branca" ["White Wing"] on the harmonica. The first version is traditional and sounds like the Luís Gonzaga recording; then all is converted into a "blues" style. Mike Grossman says Flávio is the best in all Brazil and this is ample evidence to prove it! Then Flávio plays a song with Téo Azevedo, a combination of "cantoria" and blues; Grossman thinks this type of new combination of unexpected music has a future in Brazil and will later produce albums of such stuff.

Then the "cattle call" singers ["boiadores"] perform; it is really pretty and reminds me of the rhythm and even the sound of Luís Gonzaga and perhaps a little of Gerardo Vandré's iconic "Disparada." This is followed by improvisation of verse by the singer-poet Louro Branco accompanied by a friend and both do a "mote" or verse honoring the "gringo" present. Then Téo Azevedo interviews me for about ten minutes (it was no big deal but turned out all right).

I feel sorry for the only "cordel" poet present, Ulysses Higino (what a name!); he sells "cordel" poems from the Luzeiro Publisher in São Paulo and has two or three with them. He had a poetry improvisation ["uma glosa"] all prepared but there is not time on air to do it. Again, out of social necessity but not necessarily personal interest I buy some CDs and tapes from the singer-poets. Ulysses' story-poem over the impeached Brazilian President Collor de Mello (1990) will appear in my book "História do Brasil em Cordel." (As they say "There is nothing new under the sun:" Dilma's predicament in 2016 mirrors a little the scandal and corruption of Collor de Mello in 1990.)An Aside: in the radio studio I was able to hear all the spoken Portuguese and understand almost all of it, no small feat since this was "pure" Northeastern accent and lexicon.

After the show all the group except for Michael Grossman and Flávio repaired to the "Northeastern hangout," ["o cantinho nordestino"] and invited me to the big lunch or "almoço." It was a nostalgic return to the Northeast: we dined on "carne de sol com farofa, arroz e feijão mulato." I thoroughly enjoyed being with the "cantadores" and "boiadores;" one of them could have been the twin brother of old friend Marcus de Atayde of Recife in 1966-1967. An Aside: Marcus was a guide, informant and interpreter at times for me in Recife and Pernambuco then; he is one of the many sons of one of the most important poets of all time of "cordel," João Martins de Atayde and his publishing domain from 1920 to the late 1950s. I wrote extensively of the famous poet in "Adventures of a "Gringo" Researcher in Brazil in the 1960s.

The poets and singers at the lunch were from Alagoas and Bahia. I recounted my adventure in 1967 on the sternwheeler on the São Francisco River and the wild ride (I was hitchhiking with a couple of would-be playboys from the São Francisco Navigation

Company) from Xique-Xique along the river to Salvador. Ha ha. Their girlfriends and/ or wives were present, one of them a nurse in São Paulo. It was like the old days in the boarding house in Recife, the infamous "Rose House" ["Chácara das Rosas"]. "I swear: "I really get along well with these people!"

Then came the "show" featuring "Heleno dos 8 Baixos" on the soundbox; it was all "forró" music and everyone was dancing. Really a lot of fun. About that time I began thinking how in the heck was I going to leave and find my way "home" to Abigail and Ze's house a long way from there. I caught a taxi, paid USD $11 to get to the city center and there knew how to catch a bus back "home." It turned out to be a memorable experience to be on the radio, not for me, but for that "cast" of popular northeastern culture; the experience has never been repeated. Curiously, because I was already so familiar with the "cordel" and the singer-poets' improvisations, the parts that really appealed to me were the "cattle calls" and the sound box music, something different and new.

Opening of the conference at USP and sessions at the conference

This turned out to be not as exciting as the radio performances already described, but I must admit that, as on many other occasions, it was my academic talk and attendance at the conference that paid the majority of expenses for this stay in Brazil. Tonight was the opening of the conference held in the "salão nobre" of USP and there was a full house; I ended up like many others watching and hearing the proceedings via TV in another room. It was not too pleasant as I recall hearing some horribly boring academic presentations via that small TV screen. The traditional welcome cocktail party was later and I had a good time with some history students, arriving home at 3:00 a.m.!

On another day I went to another conference location in the downtown and it all began with a quick view of the program. There were "guests" like I was in Recife in 1988 and João Pessoa in 1989 and "the less important" who read papers; I was one of the latter and would present a talk at a session at 4:15 with a session title I did know as of yet. Who was I to complain? The talk to be read and the conference paid for the trip, and I should not forget what was accomplished: the signed contract with EDUSP for my best book to that point via the contact with Sérgio Miceli. But I wrote of the conference and the talks: "Boring." And I think I was not alone in this opinion; at this point in the career that whole process of reading papers was, well, a bit tiresome.

I'm going downtown this evening for the autograph party for Jerusa Pires' new book and I anticipate I shall see the literary crowd from São Paulo. I hitched a ride with Biga and Zé Rubens and Ricardo, the latter going to a karate class and Biga and Zé going to see his 83 year old mother.

The book party was at the "Belas Artes" bookstore. The highlight for me was meeting once again José Aderaldo Castelo one of my Brazilian intellectual heroes from the 1960s whose books I always respected. Jerusa asked me to telephone her the next day. Edilene

Matos showed up and it was a happy reunion; I was glad to see her after the Bahia days. I managed to save the day for food with a sandwich of ricotta and a cold beer at a "pé sujo" to the side of the bookstore. I've got a big map of São Paulo and am trying to orient myself in this huge metropolis, but it is not an easy task. On another day there was a bit of an adventure trying to exchange money; I went to a bank which turned out to be closed, returned later and they did not accept dollars. I caught a bus to a big shopping center, the El Dorado, and finally succeeded in exchanging dough.

Michael Grossman and the Singer-Poets" and Assis Ângelo

There was a visit with Michael to an art gallery, "Artes do Interior;" the owner was his girlfriend Sílvia Inês Antônio; the art was similar to some seen in the Northeast, yet different.

It was time to talk of Michael's business: Export-Import. It was a bit difficult to figure it all out, that is, the day to day operations of the business. Later we would have a good session at his apartment seeing his collection of Blues. His father was from Belgium and arrived in Brazil in 1939 and stayed. Mike studied in São Paulo and at Columbia University in New York; he loved Brazil but said his heart was in New York. He was involved with some project with the drummer from the Rolling Stones and was doing recordings combining Brazilian Music with the poetic duels ["desafios"] of the singer-poets.

Mike arranged a meeting for me with Assis Ângelo, the cultural icon of Northeastern Culture in São Paulo; Assis does articles for the papers and has a major TV program. He also works on Rádio Atual and has been a journalist in São Paulo for twenty years. He and I spent that afternoon drinking beer in a "pé sujo" near his apartment, and I guess that cemented the relationship since we found we had much in common. We traded stories about experiences in research in the Northeast and life there. I felt totally "at home" with Assis who is originally from João Pessoa but has lived in São Paulo for years, the epitome of the "nordestino" who has made it in the South. He is central to the movement of northeastern culture in São Paulo and has had his radio program for years, but does lots of other things (like a true Brazilian intellectual). He makes his real living ["o ganha-pão"] as an administrator for the Metrô of São Paulo. He is an incredible character, a living encyclopedia of the Northeast and Northeasterners in São Paulo, pioneer and true "survivor" from the Northeast. He reminded me very much of good friend Sebastião Nunes Batista and the latter's role in Rio de Janeiro at the Fair of São Cristóvão and his job at the Casa de Rui Barbosa.

Encounter with Sízio Araújo and his family, relatives of Clarice Deal of ASU

Sízio Araújo, Clarice's brother and his family

Mark, Sízio and family

I spoke by phone with Araújo, Clarice's brother, and would see them one of those days. It turned out I hitched a ride with Abigail that turned into a somewhat wild ride on the freeway to the district of Santo Amaro. Biga was driving, got lost, but we were helped out by a taxi driver who showed us the way. A pleasant evening ensued with beer and pizza, good talk with Sízio, Theresa his wife and their boys Douglas and Gláuber.

Signing the book contract at the University Press of São Paulo and the conference once again

I made the trip to the USP Press and signed the contract with Sérgio's assistant Marcelo; Sérgio is in the U.S. for a month. But we dotted all the I's with Plínio Martins who really would do the book, now with a new title. I was to send the images, a new "conclusion" along with the new title, and a new end to the book featuring the impeachment of Collor de Mello. They wanted an autobiographical page at the end. Plínio wanted me to come for the publishing party. I never went, but am not sure why; I think they decided it was not necessary or perhaps too big an expense. The moment was totally efficient and quick: I signed three copies of the contract and said goodbye to EDUSP.

Later that day I went to the SOLAR or main auditorium of USP and heard a fine talk by Darcy Ribeiro; his talk reminded of the meeting in Rio in 1973 but he was far less bombastic than the Portuguese or the Bahians!

Then there was a very different and unique night with Mike Grossman and his girlfriend Nara: we listened to music from Buddy Guy (whom I would grow to appreciate later on in the Blues Scene in Chicago), the Rolling Stones, and Muddy Waters. Mike had a video of one of Buddy's studio sessions from Germany in 1962 and was insistent on linking the Blues with those poetic duels ["cantorias"] from the singer-poets in Brazil, a fact already mentioned but which bears repeating. He had contacts in Las Vegas, Mississippi, the guitarist from the Rolling Stones and Flávio of the "Blues Etilicos." This obviously was not my crowd but was an education for the ole' "cordel" folklorist and Kansas farm boy. Nara his "noiva" had a gallery for twenty years in Recife and now for ten years in São Paulo. She knew Brennand and Samico, colleagues of Ariano Suassuna. We enjoyed drinks, smokes and blues!

A meeting with Jerusa Pires at her home in São Paulo

I arrived at Jerusa's house on another day; she had forgotten the date (maybe it was another of those Brazilian invitations of "Come on over to the house some time" ["Venha lá em casa"]) but we made the best of it. She is a major figure in the university-literary scene in São Paulo. She let me peruse her "cordel" collection, a bit unorganized but of high quality in regard to the 32 page "romances de cavalaria," her main interest in the poetry. She wanted an eight page article from me on "Cordel" and World War II. Because I had not yet published "História do Brasil em Cordel" and this was an important topic in that coming book, I guess I feared the possibility of plagiarism, not necessarily from her but from other Brazilians who "are wont" to do such things, so I was hesitant. I thought however, "Eight pages can do no harm." We had lunch with her husband Boris Sneiderman (Russia to São Paulo).

An Aside: I later changed money once again in the Shopping Center noting that travelers' checks are exchanged for only about 90 per cent of their value, a good lesson. In the future I would use cash and perhaps a credit card.

Events to come in São Paulo

It was another morning at the USP. My talk was programed for 4:00 p.m., a lousy time usually filled by "assistant professors." I fulfilled the obligation and returned home to pack bags and catch a taxi to Guarulhos; there would be much to share at home.

That night. I went with Biga and Zé Rubens to the bus station to leave one of the boys who was traveling to Brasília; the "gringo" experienced the São Paulo beltway and the Via Dutra on the ride. The highlight of the evening was the dinner they treated me to at the "Restaurante Canelo" in the "Jardins" district where we ate pizza, "frango à passarinho" (one of my favorites in Brazil), and drank cold draft beer. It was a great evening and I slept well.

On the next day there was another morning session at the conference at the USP. I could not force myself to hear any more academic talks and skipped out to the Humanities Library which had ventilator fans and was a bit cooler. Lunch was with a professor from Leeds and Professor Lehman from Cambridge; Lehman's session that p.m. turned out to be of lesser interest to me at this point in the academic career.

Then came my session – what a joke! First of all, not all the scheduled participants showed up; one who did was a graduate assistant and there was one more brave soul, a political activist and pro-abortion leader. The latter works with USP and with Plínio Martins in the publishing house. It all turned out as well as could be expected; I was disappointed to be in the "graduate assistants'" session for beginners. We chatted a few minutes about the talk and then all "split the scene." A little humility is a good thing.

That night there was a long ride to the airport where I checked in, bought some souvenirs including Brazilian chocolates, and it was time to leave.

Reflecting and conclusions, the trip to São Paulo

The "service" on ole' Varig was not the same: no travel folders or maps, no sleep mask ["tapa-oíhos"], no slippers nor welcome drink. But yes, there was a travel toothbrush! The meal was okay but I had little appetite; there was time to reflect and record these thoughts.

First was the incredible shock of that first day in Rio: the most absolute poverty on the highway from the international airport to the downtown and South Zone. All the streets seemed to be torn up, construction of the Rio subway extensions. Life seemed to be much more difficult in Brazil. I'm like the poets of "cordel" and their mantra: "Oh Tempora. Oh Mores" ["Ah, the good ole' days"]. But much was the same: the icy "choppe" at the beach, the sea itself. I had to decide if all this was because I was 54 years old and not 24 like that first trip to Brazil! The traffic was worse, no doubt. The old charm of Rio still existed but it was a bit harder to discover it.

The encounters with Roberto, my former student, were excellent, especially the night when we listened to the "choro" group in Flamengo. (Most of the music I hear in Brazil today does not excite me.)

São Paulo. My god! The city was massive and it was a challenge. The districts of the Jardins, Higienópolis and others reminded me of Rio's south zone without the beach.

There were moments when the Portuguese did not come easily, I think it was because too much time had passed since the last visit to Brazil, but all in all I did "okay," if not great. I probably did best with the time with Heitor, Sérgio and Plínio at the USP press and at "Rádio Atual" with the northeasterners. Strangely enough I understood the singers-musicians well at the lunch at the Northeastern Cultural Center with all the background noise. And I was able to communicate well with my talk at the conference.

The time spent with Michael Grossman and Nara Roesel – it was not my world but just the same I truly enjoyed it. Mike was the epitome of the "free spirit;" I never met anyone so linked to and enthusiastic about the blues! He treated me well, and once again, he thrived on linking diverse things – U.S. Jazz, the "Blues Etílicos," the guitarist with the Rolling Stones and Flávio the Harmonica master.

An Aside from the flight home: Varig is now selling I don't know what all after the meal; it's turning into an Egyptian bazaar!

Abigail was a great person, hardworking and with a killing schedule. Zé Rubens was something else, very "simpatico," but with touches of that old Brazilian "machismo" I think. He would leave home and go to Matto Grosso "to fish." She was left in São Paulo with the academic world, all serious business for her. The kids seemed like typical teenagers to me. Their hospitality and kindness were once again amazing in my experience over the years in Brazil.

A final note: professionally it was all a great success at the EDUSP in São Paulo. That conference at Brown University in 1994 was the catalyst for it all; that plus my "salesmanship" for the project with Heitor at the USP. They were going to do a great job (and they did!). This time there would be a high quality book! (Sales over the years proved this point.)

Another Airline Aside: the stewardess on this flight is Japanese-Brazilian; she radiates personality.

The heat and the humidity created problems for me; it will take a few days to recuperate.

A note: I laughed a lot on this trip to Brazil, in Rio and in São Paulo.

Ruminating on the future at ASU

I find no magic solution for the classes at ASU. Should I teach the "cordel," but to whom? A more recent memory: I think that in the last year at ASU in 2002 before retirement I did indeed do a course on the "cordel" and it came out well and with good students! I'm very tired; I spent two hours on the flight doing these notes (a custom on return flights from Brazil, the best time to gather thoughts).

And once again, all this makes me appreciate the relatively easy life we have at home and the comforts there. I do not understand well what is going on right now with the Brazilian economy. I only know we would have a tough time surviving there.

End of the trip. 1996.

CHAPTER VI

TRIP TO BRAZIL 2000 – THE BRASA CONFERENCE IN RECIFE

Reasons for the Trip

It will be a research trip once again, the last with the Varig Air Pass which I used quite a lot and with success.

The flight

Departing Phoenix on Delta, 2000

The plane for Rio is an MD – 11 gigantic in size and now at the beginning of the flight I am finally feeling some enthusiasm for the trip. Delta was fine this time, equal to the modern Varig, a drink, salad, rice, beef, chocolate cake and "cafezinho," all good.

I slept little and we were brusquely awakened at 4:30 a.m. for breakfast. There was a wait of two hours at the São Paulo airport (this flight was Dallas, São Paulo, Rio) but arriving in Rio there was the usual combination of clouds, fog and pollution, green light at customs, changing $20 and the "frescão" bus to the California Othon Hotel.

Arrival in Copacabana and the first days in Rio with Roberto Froelich

The bus ride was the same, the new freeway passing by São Cristóvão, Rio Branco, Candelária, Santos Dumont, Glória, Flamengo and all of a sudden Copacabana!

The arrival in Copacabana

The small hotel was fine; I tried to sleep but there was a big tennis tournament on TV and the sound reverberated from I don't know where with the hero Guga winning. I walked a bit on the "calçada" of Copacabana and went back to the room to see the Los Angeles Lakers on TV.

I telephoned former student Roberto Froelich and left a message and then the wife of old friend Henrque Kerti (deceased); Cristina seemed happy I was in the city. There is news: Letícia married Rodrigo, the son of Glória Pérez, mother of Daniella of fame as Jasmine in the "telenovela" "Corpo e Alma" on TV Globo. Cristina manages the family restaurant in Barra and wants me to visit and also see Letícia and Rodrigo.

As usual I felt the shock of the change: Rio is gigantic, the traffic is scary, and I almost felt like it was my first time in the city. Copacabana seemed the same; I felt like a "gringo." I found my old hangout and tasty food place, the "Braseiro" (the same since 1967) and had a dinner of "bife, vinagrete, e batata frita" washed down with a cold beer. This was followed by the tasty "cafezinho" at the bar to the side of the hole in the wall café.

"Keah, once again I wish you were here; Rio would be great for a long weekend. I don't know if you would feel comfortable; you have to be patient. Homesick for you; the photos help."

I slept until 8:30 a.m. and then the racket started, someone hammering outside my hotel window. The breakfast is buffet style: "café com leite, queijo de Minas, abacaxi, suco de laranja e pão francês." I walked to Roberto's house but he was not at home, so I walked down to the beach in Leme and out to Fishermen's Rock. There was an interesting conversation with a guy who had spent thirty years in Amazonas State and was a fierce critic of the U.S. (the same line of thought as in the 1960s). He said Chico Mendes "never worked a day in his life."

A detour to Rocinha

I had a draft beer at the beach and then came an unexpected adventure. I caught the Leme-Gávea Bus number 592 wanting to get to the far end of Leblon Beach. It passed through Botafogo, Jardim Botânico, and the Jóquei Club and then turned right and began to climb the hill, climbing through many curves to the top of Gávea with the passengers blacker as we moved along. It turns out we had passed through the middle of Rocinha, at that time the most infamous "favela" of Rio, known for the drug gangs and violence. I managed to remain calm, the only white person on the bus, perhaps remembering the old Catholic prayer, "Angel of God ..." and rode the bus down the hill on the other side of the "favela" and changed to another down below. This one passed through the "Dois Irmãos Tunnel," Leblon, Ipanema and on over into Copacabana. Rocinha on that sunny day seemed poor, full of people in the streets and the epitome of what should be a Samba School district of Rio. There are no photos, but I shall remember the ride!

It's back to the "Braseiro" for "contra-filé, fritas, farofa, vinagrete, duas cervejas e espresso." The stomach is acting up however and it's a two-Pepto Bismal day.

Back at the hotel for a nap, Roberto Froelich called and I'll see him tonight. And Cristina Kerti called; we will go to the restaurant tomorrow night. Tomorrow is also Vasco versus Flamenco and the city is excited at the prospect ["está fervendo"].

Encounter with Roberto, "The Western Canon" and the Northeastern Market

Roberto Previdi Froelich, "The Western Canon"

Roberto came to the hotel and we went to the "Sindicato do Choppe" until 3:30 in the morning! It was chicken stew for me taking care of my stomach. The reunion was great; the reader may recall that Roberto was best student of all time in Portuguese at ASU - He went to Brazil and stayed! He is 38 years old now but seems the same. He has absolutely incredible Portuguese, does technical translating and teaches English to executives. He lives in the same place as described in 1996. He now has a girlfriend, Fátima. He is "spiritual," but not religious, believes in Reincarnation; Roberto later will convert to Brazilian Kardec Spiritism, heart and soul. And Buddhism! His family left Phoenix and now lives in Houston. We talked about the old days and Literature at ASU. Roberto is now a fan of Harold Bloom, an anti-critic from Harvard who condemns all traditional literary criticism in the U.S. in his book "The Western Canon." Roberto told of the gossip at ASU and did all of his terrific imitations of all the old professors, including Curran. Conclusion: Father Mazza of Saint Louis University was right: Curran is the epitome of the naïve.

An Aside: The city "está fervendo" today; it is the Carioca Soccer Championship between Vasco and Flamengo. Roberto said he would go to the stadium (Maracanã) except for the violence. I recalled that I went to the same championship game but in 1966 with Henrique Kerti – it was Flamengo versus Bangu, my first time in the Maracanã. See the book "Adventures of a 'Gringo' Researcher in Brazil in the 1960s" for details of that now famous game.

Roberto accompanied me to São Cristóvão and the Fair. It now consists principally in beer stands and "forró" music, all of them competing in a tremendous wall of noise. The fair seemed much smaller, "decharacterized" ["descaraterizado"] as the folklorists like to say. There was only one small "cordel" stand, that of Expedito da Silva and his woodcut artist son Erivaldo. I left the fair thinking I would never return. There are huge ramifications for me, as one might expect: it is the end of an era of "povão e pobreza."

Ups and downs. My stomach was giving me such fits that I cancelled the meeting for later that day with Roberto and went to the hotel to try to rest. There were negative emotions after the visit to the fair: I thought of leaving "cordel" research after retirement from ASU and doing something totally different in retirement. The challenge is to adapt to this new reality: the end of the "cordel" era, at least as it seemed to me in 1990. (All would change for the better later.)

Cristina called and will pick me up and we shall go to the restaurant. The status of my stomach is not good but we shall see; there is an encounter programed for tomorrow with Roberto and COMIDA BAHIANA!

Encounter with Cristina Kerti and family

Mark, Rodrigo, Letícia and Cristina in the restaurant in the Barra

Cristina picked me up at 10 p.m.; we drove for some time to the Barra district, that new area of Rio noted for its luxury and life for the upper class (the condominiums with pools back from the beach and lots of security). We passed through Copacabana, around the "Lagoa Rodrigo de Freitas," three tunnels, though São Conrado and finally to Barra. It seemed like it was all tall condos, "shoppings" and "Made in the U.S.A." I met the newlyweds Letícia and Rodrigo in the restaurant; she told stories of American Field Service days in Oklahoma ("You can take the girl out of Rio, but you can't take Rio out of the girl"). She is about to take the law school exams to practice in Rio. Cristina's friend Marta is a criminal defense lawyer in the city, and to top it off, Rodrigo is a lawyer as well.

The restaurant is a "churrascaria" so we dined on: "palmito, batata "romanoff" ótima, picanha, choppe e banana flambé." We talked a little of the past and I saw photos of Rodrigo and Letícia's wedding. There were many bridesmaids (recall the bachelorette party in the Scenarium Night Club in Rio in 2016 with the table full of the same, all beautiful Cariocas!) and it took place in an old church in the city, the one with the huge silver altar (the same where Henrique and Cristina were married). The reception was in the Copacabana Palace Hotel. Cristiano, Henrique's brother fulfilled the role of the "father of the bride" in Henrique's absence. Cristina says she is still recuperating from paying all the bills. She wanted to know all about my interest in a project on Glória Pérez (the "folhetos" covering the whole lurid story of Daniella's death). I showed the photos of you and Katie and they of course wanted to know once again why Keah and Katie never came with me to Brazil. "Maybe next time! You can count on it. This is indeed another world." My stomach survived and I rested well, going to bed at 1:00 a.m. and getting up at 9:30, early!

On another day I had breakfast someplace in Copacabana, don't know exactly where: fried eggs, orange juice, bread and butter and good "café com leite." It was a beautiful day, sunny but not too hot.

The results: Flamengo 3, Vasco 1.

Lunch at Roberto's house. My stomach is only so-so; lunch was "arroz, feijão preto, peixe frito, e salada." There was good conversation. Roberto really knows his literature; he thinks the theories of the major critics are "pompous" and likes Harold Bloom and "The Western Canon." We spoke of the principal works of Spain and Brazil. He is open to seeing the value of "cordel" and promised to take it seriously. I spoke of the thesis of the future book "História do Brasil em Cordel" and he seemed to appreciate it. On the other hand Roberto converted me to show more of an interest in Brazilian "futebol" which I admit I have rather ignored over the years. The most important: I left feeling good about our friendship, my work and my contribution to Brazil.

I had an appointment to go to Glória Pérez's office but TV Globo called her: there is an emergency, the sequester of a city bus and all its passengers near the Botanical Gardens; it is all on national television live, a drama of national crime. She is needed to report.

Then came my last visit to the "Braseiro" for "galeto no espeto, legumes e arroz." I wrote, "I have had no contact with all the famous culinary spots in Rio over all these years and feel no remorse. Such spots as "O Braseiro" are just fine."

The next day I got up early, having slept little for no reason at all (Possibly stress? The logistics of the trip?) There was breakfast in the hotel and then I paid the bill and dragged my luggage to the other side of Avenida Atlântica to catch the "frescão" to the Galeão. There were lots of folks doing their walking along the "calçada" (the British called this old regime of exercise "Fazer Cooper"]. Twenty minutes later the bus arrived and we did a slow roll through the south zone to the downtown and on out to the airport.

Conclusions of the stay in Rio

The city seemed the same as ever; "Keah, if you were with me it would be better." It always takes time for me to adjust once again to life here in this city which is enormous. I accomplished a lot during these four days, but the traffic and the pollution were horrible. I have the impression that Rio is a city now where people live in fear. One can ignore this atmosphere and you really have to do that.

Roberto is astonishing: he really has turned into a "Carioca," once again the case of my most successful student over the years. He feels no fear in Rio, a result he says of his Buddhism. The people in Leme call him by his first name in the streets! (I should recall that some years later I had the great pleasure of re-connecting with Larry Johnson, another great success among my past Portuguese students, but in an all-together different world: business and the "Fogo do Chão" restaurants.)

On the other hand Rio is making a great effort to still be that "cidade maravilhosa" – the sidewalks are clean and people carry little bags to clean up after their pets now. There is life on the streets, in the bars, cafés, and restaurants, and it seems like a lot of people are having a lot of fun. I even found myself wanting calm and a bit of silence and asked myself if the growth in Rio could continue? Roberto calls me old-fashioned and an "antiquarian" and he's right. My world here in Brazil except for the "canon" of traditional writers, is over ["já era"]. Also my music. The "favelas" are growing and the commercial sector seems older and run-down. I have the impression the rich live in luxury, but like in prison behind their walls, with guards who keep the criminals and other Brazilians out!

But the beach, "futebol," and carnival continue!

Leaving the "new" Galeão, 100 per cent antiseptic, it seemed almost like a "virtual" airport. "Brazil the land of contrasts" is not just a cliché!

I think my book "Retrato do Brasil em Cordel" is not going to describe just "cordel" or the Northeast but is going to reflect a time, a place, values and a moment (one century) in history. It really is a portrait, certainly not of a paradise, but in one sense a better world than now: "Oh Tempora! "Oh Mores" "Things were better before." Such say the poets of "cordel."

I got the last seat on the airplane and thought I would vomit from the pizza Varig served (lunch used to be good beef). The airplane impressed me: How clean! How prosperous! How non-Brazilian it seemed!

Arriving in Salvador

From the hotel in Barra, Salvador

Sunset at Barra Beach

What a pleasure to see the horizon without pollution, the blue sky and coast of Salvador. I got the old "frescão" bus to my hotel, following all along the sea coast leading into the city ["a orla"], all very familiar to me. Note that the cost of the bus was 2.1 "reais;" a taxi would have been at least 50. I sat in the old bus seat and just enjoyed the ride; the water of the sea was beautiful but not yet that of the blue-green of summertime. All the new construction along the "orla" was astounding with the high rises and such but the bay was still as beautiful as ever.

I'm on the eighth floor of the hotel with a beautiful view of Barra Beach, recalling those days of 1966 when we left "A Portuguesa" boarding house on Avenida 7 near Piedade Plaza and hopped the bus down to the Barra, went for a swim, and then had a terrific lunch at the "Portuguesa" restaurant just off the beach. A twenty minute swim in the cold water of the hotel pool helped to revive me from the trip from Rio. I'm not ready to go to the beach alone just yet; lunch served in room service was tasty and quite reasonable; I'm not ready to eat alone in the restaurant, not just yet anyway.

I spoke by phone to Carlos Cunha at the Academy of Letters of Bahia and he seemed happy to hear my voice. We set up a meeting for the next day, he already wanting me to go to a book party. We shall see.

I spoke to Mário Barros; I will see them Saturday in Itapuã for the beach and lunch. "Keah, if you were here we would do some tourism, folklore shows and maybe a boat trip to the Island of Itaparica through The Bay of All Saints." The sea is beautiful. Mário and Laís's son, Eduardo, is on a "trek" of six days to the Diamantina region, a total of 75 kilometers and sleeping in a camp tent. Laís is completing exams at the University in family therapy.

That night I slept poorly and it turned out to be a bit of a crazy day. Breakfast was: coconut yogurt, pineapple, abacaxi, scrambled eggs, good bread and "café com leite."

"Hanging Out" in Salvador: the São Francisco Church and the "Fundação Casa de Jorge Amado"

The São Francisco "Plaza," Salvador

Mark with the Franciscan friar

I took the "executive bus" or "frescão" to the main plaza ["A Praça da Sé"]; the city seemed as interesting as back in 1966 when I first saw it: Vitória, Campo Grande, Piedade, in sum, the "cidade alta." There was little pollution and not as much heat as other times. I went to the old places: "O Terreiro de Jesus" and then a long visit to the old São Francisco church with its courtyard and the dazzling church itself; it was a calm time and I thoroughly enjoyed the lack of any hurry to appreciate it all. Then I met Frei Reinaldo, 60 years of age, and we had a very pleasant talk. We spoke of the Franciscans, the Dominicans and the Jesuits and the history of Brazil. By the way the official historian of the "Igreja de São Francisco" is Father Hugo. Reinaldo complains of the fact that there are few new vocations to the order and the bedlam of the drumming of Oludum samba club to the side of the church at night. The friar maintains the faith in the old Franciscan vision of life and that is an admirable thing. The slides I took of the church over the years are priceless (the reason is they no long allow flash photography in the church; this will of course change in later days with the advent of the digital camera.) There was time to reflect and to pray.

In the "Pelourinho" in front of the Jorge Amado Foundation

I later walked past the Third Order of Franciscans Church with its amazing façade and into the "Pelourinho," turned left past the Pierre Verger Foundation and entered the Jorge Amado Foundation. I looked over the books available for sale, including all those of Jorge Amado, and then there was a nice chat with Myriam Fraga the director who offered gifts of books from the place. Jorge Amado now is 88 years old and is in poor health; he is not receiving any visitors and according to Myriam is battling depression. (Recall my interaction with Jorge's books began in 1964 and continued with all the previous visits in Brazil, autograph parties for books and the highlight of meeting Jorge at the 50 Years of Literature Celebration in 1981. We go back a long way.) It was also good to see that the display of books included my book of 1990 on Cuíca de Santo Amaro. I felt part of something important and it was an emotional moment for me. It was worth the effort not only to do the reading and long periods of research for the book, but also the long battle to get it published (all told in a previous chapter of this book).

Edilene Matos has a new book on Cuíca; it is well illustrated but takes nothing from my book; it fact it actually complements it.

An historic Portuguese tile scene, the "Portuguese Royal Reading Room," Salvador

These tiles are indeed beautiful and mark the historic days of the sea voyages of discovery and colonization by Portugal to the East and West in the 15th and 16th centuries.

That day, after the Foundation, I had lunch alone in one of the old restaurants of the "Pelourinho" with a nice view of the Bay of Salvador. The time was spent perusing the books from Myriam; it was a calm time and a chance to remember the past. I actually enjoyed myself remembering with nostalgia those days. "Keah, it really was a moment of "weighing" past efforts and I am happy." I truly made a contribution to the intellectual life of Bahia especially taking into account I am a foreigner! All this convinced me that the effort to continue with "Retrato' must continue.

After the bus back to the hotel I spoke with friend Mário, and tried one more time to talk and link up with Carlos Cunha. Supper was at the hotel to the side of the pool: "bife, farofa, molho à campanha, cerveja fria" and I read my new book "One Thousand Brazilian Jokes" ["Mil Piadas Brasileiras"].

Another day, wandering about Salvador

I got up early and took a long walk along Barra Beach and on to the north along the "orla," passing the time talking to some fishermen.

The Lacerda Elevator facing the bay

It all started with a "frescão" to the "Praça da Sé," then the Lacerda Elevator to the Lower City (a five cent coin) and a Guaraná in the old restaurant at the top of the Mercado Modelo. There is a "cordel" stand outside the market but it offered nothing new for me. A travel anecdote: there was a young black boy working on construction on the outside veranda of the Market Restaurant; he walked the entire length of the interior of the restaurant with his large chain saw going at full speed! Only in Brazil! It seemed he passed just a little too close to my table.

A transportation note: it is fine if you take the "frescão" with its air conditioning. It all seems efficient, particularly if one avoids the traffic jams of rush hour.

A new encounter with the Barros family

I was with Mário before in 1990 and 1996; he looks good at 53 years of age. The entire conversation was in Portuguese (he is completely used to speaking to me in English and it seems perfectly normal to him). Formac is now history. Mário is working now as a consultant; he sells his expertise and charges by the hour. He mainly deals with transactions acquiring small family firms by large firms with foreign capital. He has just helped broker a deal with a large petroleum firm (8th largest in the world) which sells "seismic devices."

And he has just arranged for a firm in China to do business in Brazil (this is 2000; there will be many such ventures in the future with China expanding; it is no longer the cold war and military expansion; business accomplishes the same thing).

Mário hates traveling to Rio or São Paulo, but it is necessary and he goes often. In his view Salvador is relatively secure; the masses have good weather, "futebol," the beach, carnival and good basic foods. Recife is a little worse off but for him conditions in Rio and São Paulo are the pits!

Laís is in the Catholic University [the PUC, "Pontífica Universidade Católica"] studying family therapy; in three or four years they hope to open a small business, an office for her.

Mário's exercise is interesting: he walks each day along the "orla" for three or four hours, a 15 kilometer jaunt. His father was ill but after some good treatment is now much better. His mother is relatively good, but with aging problems as can be expected.

Eduardo is "doing his thing," trekking; he is going to launch a new WWW site for artists (painters) of Itapuã receiving a percentage of the sales for his work. He majored in sociology but likes the cultural scene more than his parents and wants to live in closer to the old city.

An aside: Mário tells me there are big plans in the works to make a "new Cancún" to the north of Salvador. Uh oh.

Mário has no regrets making the decision to live in Pedra do Sal far from the city; it is much calmer there and he can do most of his work via the phone or internet anyway.

"I spoke of you, Katie and my thinking of retiring in 2002 (it came to pass.)"

Mário says he earns well but has to depend on his "reserves. It is not as easy to travel as in the past; as the poets of "cordel" say: "The times they are getting difficult," a relative statement in regard to social class.

My hotel is good, better than the "Bahia do Sol" of past visits. I can go for exercise and walks along the beach sidewalk to the Porto da Barra. "Keah, we could enjoy a few days here." The "Pelourinho" during the day is well patrolled by the police and I don't feel any fear.

The "Igreja da Conceição da Praia" and other moments

"Nossa Senhora da Conceição da Praia" Church, lower city, Salvador

I forgot. Something new. After all these years (34 now) this morning I finally visited "A Igreja da Conceição da Praia" in the lower city, the first of the many churches in all the city. It was calm and good for the soul; this is the famous church that is the point of departure for all the "Bahianas" dressed in regional finery for the pilgrimage and long walk to the Church of Jesus of the Good End" ["Igreja do Jesus do Bom Fim"] famous for the Brazilian syncretism, the mixture of Catholic and African religions. The "Bahianas" wash the steps entering the church in homage to the African "Bom Jesus" and there is a Catholic mass held inside. (I had a wonderful visit to this church in 2014 while on staff for Lindblad-National Geographic Expeditions.)

That night: once again I had dinner by the pool with my "1000 Brazilian Jokes" keeping me company. There was a nice talk with a gentleman from the oil district of Bahia at Pojuca. TV was much the same: good ole' Leonel Brizola of the distant political past is still around and making waves in the recent elections.

The next morning there was a long walk of some forty minutes by the "Cristo Redentor;" the sea was beautiful; there were tide pools and birds, the best of Bahia. It was also relatively cool; followed by a shower and the "frescão" to the city.

Mário, Carlla, and Laís Barros

An anecdote from the Barros: their cook's sister cooked for the Pope and then for some upper crust folks in São Paulo.

An anecdote of life in Bahia. Carjacking-robberies are common now. The thieves make you drive to your ATM machine, stop the car, get out and withdraw cash. Mário told of one time when a friend told him that the thief wanted to do the transaction himself, got the number, jumped out of the car to go to the machine; the driver just drove off. Laughter.

Mário is going to Venezuela soon for a business deal involving petroleum; he hates Caracas which he terms "a poor Bahia."

I have the impression everyone in Salvador now uses a cell phone, including the poor people. All that is except this "gringo."

Carla now has her BSBA degree and a good job but Mário says the economy is really unstable. He believes the future is the internet: a client in Europe makes a purchase; an agent in the U.S. manufactures the product. Everything is "off-shore," thus avoiding taxes. It appears that all this will become a "photo" of business in the future in Brazil and the world. What is a poor folklorist-writer on "cordel," a language and literature professor, to do?

The arrival in Recife and the BRASA Conference in the year 2000

The hotel in Recife, Piedade Beach ["Praia da Piedade,"] the BRASA Conference

In the hotel the first person I recognized was Idelette Mozart the researcher from France I had met in João Pessoa in 1989; she said it was a pleasure to see me again. The view from my room on an upper story is beautiful of the "Praia da Piedade," and the hotel has all the amenities. A ferocious cold started in Recife; it may be the climate change in Recife, but Roberto was at the end of one in Rio and Laís in the middle of one in Salvador. This one will be a doozy! On the other hand, my stomach is fine for the moment.

I saw Ricardo Paiva from Georgetown and Jon Tolman from New Mexico University, the head of BRASA (have I said that is the Brazilian Studies Association?). Paiva wants me to do an introduction for a talk during lunchtime tomorrow. More later, it was a farce.

I bought ampicillin, aspirin and Cepacol; I can't miss that flight on Friday. It does not help that the lobby of the hotel is freezing from the air conditioning and so is the room, but I was at least able to figure out the room control and warm it up.

The opening night of the conference

We all went by bus to the Convention Center which is located at the Federal University campus: the auditorium was like an icebox; I had my chamois shirt buttoned to the throat to try from turning into an icicle. This is not the first time it has happened over the years in Brazil. It is amazing to me how these folks from a serious tropical climate can possibly stand that frigid air; it may have something to do with wanting to have first world air conditioning in a country aspiring to be first world. The first speaker was Marcus Accioly, writer and journalist and number one speaker here after Ariano Suassuna. The speech was "Brazilian Baroque" (recall my description of the Conference of 1973 in Rio).

Then there was music by the "Quinteto Violado" of fame in the 1970s, an integral part of the "Movimento Armorial;" the show was excellent with northeastern "baião" and regional dances but at approximately ten times the necessary volume (another Brazilian custom akin to the air conditioning already described). I actually had to take a break from the auditorium due to a splitting headache and the cold. They did play one of my all-time favorites: "Disparada" from Gerardo Vandré (recall the National Festivals of Music of the MPB ["Música Popular Brasileira"] on national television from 1967 on with Chico Buarque, Jaír Rodrígues, Nara Leão and Vandré among the favorites). They also played excerpts from the "Missa do Vaqueiro" of the times. There were two sets of drums at maximum volume; such were the times. I noted that Ariano Suassuna, the main invited guest in the audience, left after only two or three songs. It was surprising that the majority of the "congressistas" actually stayed until the end.

I made a welcome new friendship with Edson Oliveira of São Paulo; we ate "crepes" and drank a cold beer after the concert. He researches the Xavante natives and does translations from their language to Portuguese. I also met Jackson, a sociologist from Ceará but it was all very difficult with this terrible throat and cold coming on.

The medical doctor and the luncheon

I spent the next morning preparing for the introduction of Dr. Jaír Figueiredo, a urologist from Natal, Rio Grande do Norte State, and according to Paiva, "an expert on 'cordel.'" "You go with the flow." He is known for opening conferences on medicine with readings from "cordel" - like story-poems he has written on AIDS. He told me the "folhetos" are then distributed by the State and to this point 800,000 have been printed! (The amazing number is correct). This is not entirely new to "cordel;" there were cases as far back as the 1960s when the poets were paid to write about the dangers of tuberculosis and such, but on a far lesser scale than this. You can imagine me muttering under my breath and talking to myself comparing this to the true "cordel" and famous poets of the past.

So I found myself in a horrendous situation. The doctor's talk was scheduled during lunch time. It turns out no one was particularly interested, after all, they were there to eat, renew old acquaintances, and "network" for new ones, so the talk was pretty much ignored and drowned out by the conversation at all the tables. Aside from that the microphone was a disaster. I actually felt a bit chagrined having any part of it. One good thing: during the lunch I renewed an acquaintance with Francisco de Mattos a scholar, writer and professor at the Federal University of Pernambuco. He was familiar with my work, having taught at the University of Arizona in Tucson, visiting ASU in Tempe and knew about my study on Ariano Suassuna.

A new low point: the throat was so bad that I tried to gargle with some aspirin and about vomited from the taste. I am feeling a bit better now but don't know if I will be able to give my scheduled talk tomorrow. There was chicken soup from room service tonight and orange juice as I write these notes. Tomorrow will be an important day and with some stress; I am scheduled to eat lunch with the "cordel" group and Ariano Suassuna.

I signed up for a city tour on another day; hope I can make it with this nasty cold.

"Keah, I read your Father's Day card and admit there was a tear or two; I am feeling very loved and hope this goes on the same for the next twenty-five years."

The next day I woke up at 6:00 a.m.; there was a good breakfast at the "Quebra Mar" and then the sessions. It turns out that Ariano Suassuna and his wife Zélia were present. How he stands all this I don't know but he spent the entire day.

Another day, the first session

A "crazy" professor from Minas Gerais began it all; she spoke of a single painting of Ariano's and a poem. I wrote: "This lady has diarrhea of the mouth; we are already twenty minutes behind schedule in this session."

Next was a fine professor from Rio Grande do Norte; he spoke very well about Ariano.

Then came Idelette Mozart, a first rate intellectual. An Aside: She is doing a study with one of the topics I deal with in "Bramundo" (later to become "História do Brasil em Cordel"); she found all those WW II "cordel" texts of the Guajarina press in Belém do Pará. Whose work will come out first? But her talk was fine with me, beautiful Portuguese; she has a book on Ariano and the "Movimento Armorial."

My Session – Ariano showing appreciation and the luncheon thereafter

Then my session began. A lady from Buenos Aires talked about a bad translation of Ariano's "The Rogues' Trial" ["O Auto da Compadecida"] and her own which is naturally better. A small quarrel between her and the coordinator of the session then took place, a question of how long she was going on – a bit of an irony here: the coordinator was the same person who talked so long in the first session. Question: Could it have been that the coordinator in the first session was this person from Buenos Aires? Ah, the vagaries of conference talks.

Mark speaking, Ariano Suassuna applauding

I had made a decision the night before: for the most part my presentation would have been interesting reading on paper, but not so great orally, so I tore it up. Instead, I wrote anecdotes of the research stage in Recife in 1966 in homage to Ariano. He and Zélia were in the front row of the presentation room. I did it all with just revised notes, the talk largely extemporaneous, and it was a hoot! A tremendous success. Idelette told me later: "Throw out that original talk and send me twenty pages of what you did today." Everyone was literally rolling with laughter. Ariano himself was happy, applauding and smiling. I thought: "Because it seemed entertaining perhaps I'll take

Idelette up on the idea (in fact I would do so for other reasons, this in 2001 in São Paulo). This could become a theme for next year or perhaps for the first year or two in retirement." Speaking humbling, they all truly did enjoy the talk. It was original and no one could plagiarize from it or steal the thunder. Recalling my notes of the talk: I told of the fieldwork during those first days in Recife, the "Ateliê" in Olinda, the "Chácara das Rosas" ["Sem rosas"], the São José Market and the poets, and the "innocent gringo" in the interior, in sum, the adventures of that first stage of research in Brazil.

It was later that I came up with the tentative title for the new text: "Diário de um Americano Brasilianista no Brasil." I felt like I had indeed filled the role of a pioneering researcher, albeit foreigner, in Brazil. And stretching things, after all it's my imagination, I felt a little like my literary hero João Guimarães Rosa – with those notebooks in the saddlebags of his horse as he traveled the interior as a doctor, always taking notes and writing a diary of his journeys. I would also speak in the book of the famous Brazilians I had had the good fortune to encounter in my travels. For the first time in a while I began to feel some real enthusiasm about research, all due to that reception by the audience that day. It was a moment of great happiness. Together with the talk at the "100 Years of 'Cordel'" exposition in São Paulo in coming years in 2001 this would be the most memorable talk of my career in academia. "Things seem to work out." From that year of 2000 and beyond many good things would happen until retirement (and perhaps greater things beyond that!) So this idea germinated at the BRASA meeting would go on to be the essence of the talk in São Paulo in 2001 and better yet the book published in the U.S. years later: "Adventures of a 'Gringo' Researcher in Brazil in the 1960s" ["Peripécias de um Pesquisador 'Gringo' no Brasil nos Anos 1960"].

Zélia and Ariano Suassuna

Mark, Zélia and Ariano Suassuna

At the luncheon I was seated opposite Idelette, Zélia and Ariano. Ariano's words, once again, "Thank you. I owe a lot to you sir" (referring to the quotes from the interviews with the "cordel" poets from my book of 1973 that Ariano "borrowed" for his main character "Quaderna" in "O Romance da Pedra do Reino" back in the late 1970s).

I thought in 2000: "Keep your health, a good diet and exercise. You now have a project and ideas for the future."

I recalled the themes of books already written, all academic in nature, but it was the anecdotes like these in the talk in Recife in 2000, anecdotes shared with students in the classrooms at ASU on a daily basis – these were the "meat and potatoes" of success. And along the same line anecdotes of travel in Colombia, Guatemala, Mexico, Portugal, Spain and Brazil came "alive" for the students. These anecdotes and notes from diaries would be the basis for many books to be done later during retirement.

The afternoon session: the video on Ariano Suassuna and later events

There was a film on the "Movimento Armorial" and I learned a lot. Ariano is now a "figurão," a "vulto," and "instituição" in Pernambuco and even in all Brazil. He is like Gilberto Freyre before, but much more appreciated and loved. Since my first days with him in the 1960s he is now acclaimed for his poetry, his painting, his plays, the "Movimento Armorial" and his "aulas-espetáculo".

A note with the passage of time. In 2000 I wrote of projects for the future: "Bramundo," "Retrato," "Um Brasilianista no Brasil," "Antologia em Inglês" and "The Farm." Now in 2009 they are all completed. "E, agora, Marcos?"

The Film. It was done on the occasion of Ariano celebrating his 70th birthday in 2000. It treated his father, his youth on the "Fazenda Acauã," the "cavalgadas" and "armorias," and the cattle brands using an alphabet from the new "Movimento Armorial." And he will forever be linked to "a literatura de cordel" by his "Rogues' Trial" ["Auto da Compadecida"].

An Aside: I wrote about the latter in 1969! Wow, the passage of time! I think I was the first to do so. Why? Because the "literatura de cordel" suffered from terrible prejudice in the intellectual world of the time in Brazil, and the local "heavyweights" in literary criticism did not want to either recognize it or deal with it, but fortunately not the case of writers like Jorge Amado, Ariano, Dias Gomes and a few others. However, I chose the topic and did the dissertation on it; only Ariano was aware of what I was doing; he perhaps encouraged my small book of 1973 because he saw something good in it, and coincidentally, it helped establish his own image. Today he always speaks of the link.

After the film they showed one of his "aulas-espetáculo," this one from Brasília. In it he is on a "roll" – jokes, anecdotes, illustrations from the art world, and the best: he is not hostile to other forms of art but mainly wants to maintain ferociously "what is ours." I wrote in my notes: "I am totally in agreement with him; the mass media in Brazil today including TV have totally changed and rewritten that old Brazilian reality." And I said to myself: "Don't lose faith in "cordel" as a part of Brazil's popular heritage. Old "cordel" is now pretty much gone, but I can share it in my own way and better than most."

An Aside: an older gentleman from Ceará told me in a private conversation that when he was young, in the evening everyone had their chairs out on the narrow sidewalks in front of the houses in the northeastern interior waiting for someone who could read or recite a story-poem of "cordel." Then came TV.

That night I managed a lunch from a bar across the street from the hotel and then went to the room to watch TV, still feeling weak and poorly. Tomorrow morning I will try to attend a session or two and then there is one more luncheon; I'm eating very little.

An Aside: I saw Charles Perrone again at the conference; he is a rising star in the group of "Brasilianistas" these days. I also talked with Chris Dunne from the Brown Meeting in 1994 (he would move on to Tulane), but I have really lost touch with most of that crowd. Or almost. Charles Perrone had written me a handwritten note when he was beginning at Texas and had just won a Fulbright Grant for dissertation research in Brazil, asking for advice from "the old boy." I write of this now just to show the different "generations" of researchers at the conference.

Tourism in Recife and Olinda and the "Sá Grama" concert

The "4ᵗʰ of October Hotel," Recife

Mark, the cardboard tourist mockup of the bandit Lampião

That afternoon Edson Oliveira and I took a VW bus ["piruá"] to old downtown Recife. I think it was a full 30 minutes before I could recognize anything; this was perhaps due to the fact that the conference and hotel were located on Piedade Beach, south beyond the far end of old Boa Viagem that I knew years before. We finally arrived at familiar ground: the "Conde de Boa Vista Avenue, Avenida Guararapes, Rua Imperatriz" and "Rua da Aurora," the area where I frequented all the bookstores in 1966-1967. The Rua da Aurora on the banks of the Rio Capibaribe has been all redone, the buildings painted in a pretty fashion, a bit like the remodeled "Pelourinho" in Salvador. The Historians complain, but it really is much more pleasant. The sickly beggars on the old bridge are now gone, a result of the "cleanup" ["limpeza da área"]; there used to be many beggars in rags, bloody bandages wrapped around their legs and many times one had to take care to just get by them to cross the bridge. The area is still full of street vendors selling "milho cozido, tapioca e beiju."

We walked along the river in that old area familiar to me from the past: the "Restaurante Leite" where João Pessoa was assassinated in 1930 and the "Hotel 4 de Outubro" where I spent that vivid first night in Recife in 1966. Then we went to the "Casa da Cultura," which was the old penitentiary which housed the Northeast's most famous prisoner, the old bandit Antônio Silvino of "cordel" fame and that of a model prisoner: folklore has it that through sterling behavior and his prison job he actually succeeded in putting several children through school. Only one lady had "cordel" in her shop and even then only two new "folhetos." She says the "Childrens' House" ["Casa da Criança"] in old Olinda still may have "cordel." Edson Pinto, the icon of "cordel" in the old São José Market with his decades old stand died just two months ago, a real loss to all of us. There is no reason for me to try to visit the market this trip; it is sad. See the photos of Edson and me and the caricature of Lampião. (Irony: it should be Antônio Silvino; I guess Lampião had better press.)

We caught a taxi and had a bit of a difficult time in Olinda trying to find the "Casa da Criança" which ended up being high on one of those hills, surrounded by beautiful old trees, but the building in total disrepair ["no maior abandono"]. It turns out that Delarme Monteiro one of the excellent Pernambuco poets of decades past in the Atayde Shop had a small printing shop for a while at this location, but he died some ten years ago. A little old lady told me there were still some old "folhetos" around but all were pretty much eaten by the termites! An irony: We have had to guard against the same fate for my own collection in Arizona with annual termite treatments; so far, so good. So ends the story and the end of a wild goose chase.

Olinda, view of the sea

We did a great walk through old Olinda past the "Igreja do Carmo" where we would attend a concert that night, more on that later, and then through the Olinda of the 1600s.

I think we passed by the old "sobrado" with the "ateliê" or art studio where I first lived in 1966, but so much time had passed that I can't say for sure. An Aside: Our guide on the official tour the next day (sponsored by the Conference) was Antenor, chief of planning for the preservation of Olinda by the Federal University of Pernambuco; in answer to my question he said that the artist Tiago Amorim, now 56 years old, worked for him as a counselor for youths with drug problems. Tiago was one of the principal artists of the old "ateliê" in 1966.

We climbed the hill with that famous view of far off Recife and the sea to the south of Olinda and it was as beautiful as I remembered. We spent almost two hours at the "Bar Cantinho" in the fine company of Viviana, daughter of the well-known literary critic of those days Alredo Bosi; the "choppe" flowed as did the conversation. She is an assistant professor of literary theory at the USP where she is assigned two classes, each with one hundred students, and she grades all the papers herself! She said she spent a month "at the end of the world" in Ceará, another in Amazonas State and yet another in a small city, lecturing. I thought: "She has earned her stripes." She was very kind to this "gringo."

Sérgio Campelo, his musical group "Sá Grama"

Afterwards there was one of the most pleasant nights I have spent in Brazil in the last years: it was a concert by the Sérgio Campelo group in the old baroque "Igreja do Carmo" in old Olinda. Imagine an altar totally covered in gold paint, 17th century architecture, and acoustic music! The group was comprised of ten persons, all trained in classical music but playing original compositions by Sérgio Campelo with an emphasis on northeastern regional music with northeastern regional instruments. There were three or four flutes, one "pífano" of wood, a clarinet, a "viola" of ten strings, doubled in five courses and a good classic guitar. A marimba, acoustic bass fiddle and percussion topped off the group. It was elegant! I got a bit emotional listening in my mind to the only "decent" music I have heard in Brazil on this trip. But it was more than that: it was on that small list of the most favorite music I ever heard in Brazil! There were original compositions but all based on northeastern folkloric music. "TV Globo" did a mini-series on Ariano Suassuna and this group did the background music. I was awarded two CDs of their music when they learned of my work on Ariano.

Upon returning to the hotel there was a much needed shower; Recife was like a sauna that day. I was exhausted; tomorrow will be the last day in Recife.

Visit to the art studio ["ateliê"] of Francisco Brennand

The old sugar cane mill converted into the art studio of Francisco Brennand

Master Brennand and admirers

Almost all the professors went by bus to Francisco Brennands's "kingdom." He was beginning in the 1960s when I was in Pernambuco and was a good friend and colleague of Ariano Suassuna and Samico of that intellectual "generation." The place is a museum-studio-monument to him! I had heard of him in the 1960s and do recall that at least one of his paintings was on the wall of the living room of Ariano Suassuna's house in "Casa Forte" in Recife. Brennand had become a major figure in Brazilian art and also of fame outside of Brazil. Professor Jon Tolman told me that one of his paintings sells in the neighborhood of $500,000 USD. I said, "Could it be?" Apparently so.

The last luncheon at the conference and the departure from Recife

The luncheon in Olinda, the conference participants

The visit to the "ateliê" was followed by a very pleasant luncheon in Olinda where I sat in the group of Moira Sullivan, Chris Dunne (Brown U. 1994) and Fulomena, a professor from Viséu, Portugal (Keah and I visited there in 1987.) An interesting perspective from her conversation: she hates the University of Coimbra: "It's outmoded, antiquated and useless." The menu was fish stew and rice with shrimp. Later after lunch there was a long, cultural walk through old Olinda; Antenor the guide astounded us all with his encyclopedic historical knowledge of the place. The whole time I find myself thinking of old Recife colleague, friend, and guide, Flávio Veloso; he and Antenor could have been twin brothers!

I was a bit preoccupied if all my film would make it through the machines in the airports; it turned out all right. The ride back to the hotel found me sitting to the side of the Viseu professor; concentrating and trying to understand her continental Portuguese with all the bus noise resulted in a whopper of a headache.

A bit of a final academic chat with old friends: Ricardo Paiva had heard that I was already retired (What's the old cliché: "Rumors of my retirement have been greatly exaggerated!") Tolman, of my generation and perhaps of my age, says he is tired of all the "academic bullshit," but I think he thrives on it. He did amazing work and a fine contribution to the field with his text for Portuguese, "Travessia," and his leadership for BRASA. A Curious Aside: I wrote elsewhere that one of the final academic meetings in my career at ASU was a minor meeting in Las Vegas; Jon was the chair of the session and I think there were three of us in the room. Ah, Academia! Years have passed, but in retrospect this meeting in Recife in 2000 was indeed a pleasant highlight of such moments over the years: the time with Ariano, the nostalgic return to Recife and those golden moments of music in Olinda.

That night I chose room service for dinner; I was absolutely exhausted, "This has taken a year or two off my life."

Boa Viagem, the departure

The check-out was efficient, the flight to Rio comfortable. The bookstore at the airport has my book on Rodolfo Coelho Cavalcante and the Hedra book, and the Anthology on Cuíca de Santo Amaro, all pleasing to the "ole profe."

I'm finding myself thinking of projects during retirement in 2002.

Once again there were moments during the conference when someone would approach me and say, "So you are <u>the</u> Mark Curran." My books are known, especially the one at EDUSP in São Paulo in 1998. I'm both a pioneer and current master in the "cordel" research, not bad for the farm boy from Kansas. If I had been more aggressive and Type A academically throughout the career I probably would have had many greater moments. No. It was fine. "Chega."

I'm spending time writing and reviewing this notes; I'll read them again on the airplane and then put them in a drawer for a few years until I do the retirement "memory" book. (It turns out I already have done the first one in 2009, another one two years later and now a third in 2016.) CNN News is broadcasting the big crash in the stock market today, so I'm worried about finances during retirement". An Irony: It fell in 2000 but reached a new high in 2008. Now in 2009 it's the worst since the 1929 crash and subsequent depression. And once again, at this writing in 2016 it fell again. But there is no remorse for retiring from full-time at the university in 2002; it was a good decision. All the good things that have come to pass in recent years have been a great "reward" for the career. I had more good fortune than most of my colleagues in the area. I have ideas and projects for the future and hobbies.

"Thinking of you Keah and our future, my companion, lover and spouse. All my love." June 24, "Dia de São João," 2000

CHAPTER VII

SÃO PAULO – RIO DE JANEIRO, 2001

The purpose: I was an invited speaker for the exposition of "100 Years of 'Cordel'" sponsored by SESC-POMPEIA

The flight

I left Keah feeling very poorly with bandages on face (a result of dermatologist Griego's surgeries) and on top of that, a bad cold. We were both sad.

There was some confusion about the airline ticket from Phoenix to Dallas but it got straightened out. I had a good talk on the airplane to Dallas with a federal government bureaucrat, retired in 1980; he now gives seminars on management for the "Bureau of Land Management" and other entities and has just finished one at NAU in Flagstaff. He counseled me about retirement: "Retire TO something and not FROM something."

There was a long wait in the airport in Dallas but I used the time to go over my talk for "100 Anos" and reading once again Michner's "Centennial." Fortunately there was no one to my side in my row of seats (3) on the international flight; dinner was beef, with a before dinner drink and after dinner drink, so I slept some on the long flight.

The arrival in São Paulo and the first moments

View of São Paulo and the MAS, P, Museum of Art of São Paulo 2001

On our approach to the city itself one could see the entire horizon full of skyscrapers, dim in the cloud of pollution around the city. The flight from Phoenix was two hours, twenty minutes, the flight from Dallas to São Paulo almost twelve hours.

My guide from SESC Cassia (I was an invited "special guest" for the "100 Anos" exposition and there was a team of guides contracted by SESC for this) and the chauffer met me at the airport in São Paulo. In the same VW bus ["kombi"] rode the "cordel" poet J. Barros; it is indeed a small world! He complained of ill health, his legs, and also high blood pressure. He was a good friend of Apolônio Alves dos Santos, my long-time friend and "cordel" poet from the São Cristóvão Fair in Rio; the latter now deceased for some years.

We passed through the old part of downtown São Paulo, and it seemed to me initially to be a very dirty city. The impression changed for the better a little later. The three-star hotel was just fine and calm enough, a little distant (downhill) from Avenida Paulista, the largest and most famous street in the city. Cássia had a "package" ["pacote"] for me:

the program, the schedule of events and money for meals; the balance including the honorarium would be paid Friday after my talk by the agent Sérgio. (Writing of all this in 2016 makes it all seem like a dream and I am realizing how good I had it once again in Brazil for this special event, surely another highlight of the career.)

I showered, shaved and tried to take a nap, but to no avail. I was, as usual, too exhausted and "wound up" for all this.

Introduction to the curator of "100 Anos" – Audálio Dantas

Audálio Dantas, curator of "100 Anos"

At five o'clock in the afternoon Audálio Dantas the curator of "100 Anos" in charge of the exposition picked me up at the hotel and we drove to SESC-POMPEIA. What an impressive individual! I ended up finding out all about the "great" Audálio – a reporter from my old days in Brazil in the 1960s, doing major stories for "Realidade" and "Cruzeiro" magazines, like perhaps "Time" and "Look" in the U.S.. Audálio was later elected as a "deputado" to the Brazilian House of Representatives in Brasília, Head of the Association of Journalists of São Paulo and later of the National Association of Journalists and head of the Official Press of the State of São Paulo. Wow.

"Cordel" is one of his interests but far from the main one; he is one of the major cultural figures of São Paulo.

Photo Gallery of the exposition of "100 Anos"

Cover of the catalogue, "100 Years de Cordel"

The icon of the exposition: "The Mysterious Peacock" ["O Pavão Misterioso"]

Photo of the master Leandro Gomes de Barros

Photo of Cuíca de Santo Amaro and Rodolfo Coelho Cavalcante

An "artistic" woodcut print: "The Emperor Charlemagne" ["O Imperador Carlos Magno"]

Image of the bandit Lampião and Father Cícero

Father Cícero and the icon "O Pavão Misterioso"

The exposition

The exposition was incredible; it alone made the entire trip worthwhile. My talk would be a "minor" moment. What impressed me initially was the large quantity of books, films, plays, and music in Brazil that exists as a result of the "literatura de cordel," all documented in the placards at the entrance to the exposition. I hope to document everything with slides the next few days (I did: see Gallery of Photos.)

Classic story-poems of old "cordel"

The story-poems of "cordel" itself in the glass cases of the exposition were impressive – extremely old and rare story-poems! Romances, banditry and religion were among the prominent themes. There were three hundred all together, all from the collection of the eminent researcher Joseph Luyten who actually organized all the "cordel" for curator Audálio Dantas.

They recreated in the huge space of the building an actual "fair" ["feira"] with "cordel" stands in the marketplace. Among the poets represented were J. Borges, José Lourenço of Juazeiro do Norte (from the old typography "A Tipografia São Francisco" of José Bernardo da Silva), Jerônimo Soares (brother of Marcelo Soares), Marcelo Soares, Abraão Batista of Juazeiro do Norte, Gonçalo Ferreira da Silva of Rio de Janeiro, Fanka of Juazeiro, Waldeck de Garanhuns, Téo Azevedo and Assis Ângelo. This was just the first group; the second would arrive after my departure – Azulão and others.

The decorations on the high ceiling and the walls of the enormous space were of artistic, enlarged woodcuts; there was in addition an actual "ateliê" or workshop where poets did the story-poems from beginning to end, writing the verse, cutting the wood "tacos" or wood blocks, making the woodcut prints, a small printer to print the "folheto," folding it, etc. And there were the performance spaces for the singer-poets, theater, shows and cinema. All was due to the funding of SESC-POMPEIA and the expertise of Joseph Luyten and Audálio Dantas.

Introduciton to Joseph Luyten

Joseph Luyten in his library

Joseph divides the week between Santos (the Fort and the Museum of Popular Culture) and the Methodist University ["Universidade Metodista de São Paulo]; he no longer has any connection to the USP. He has a house in Santos and an apartment in São Paulo. I will only meet him on Tuesday before the talk; notes on him follow.

I'm writing diary notes in the hotel followed by a "workout" in the small gym – ha, ha! There was time for calls to Michael Grossman, to EDUSP, some shopping on Avenida Paulista, including a new CD by the all-time favorite Chico Buarque de Holanda.

Interlude: a reencounter with Michael Grossman

I caught a taxi to Mike Grossman's house. He seemed exhausted, saying he was just with a friend from the international section of "The New York Times" or perhaps it was the "Wall Street Journal." Mike had introduced him to his future wife in Brazil.

He spoke to me of "Rádio Atual;" it turns out the owner, a federal congressman, was a thief and was just "cassado" or had his political rights taken away. So that means that the Northeastern Cultural Center I had visited on the last trip is now defunct. Téo Azevedo had left "Rádio Atual" deceived by the owner in salary matters. Assis Ângelo still has a radio program on Saturday afternoons, the most popular show on northeastern culture in São Paulo.

Mike is executive producer of the latest CD of Flávio of the "Blues Etílicos," but is more excited about the matter of Sebastião da Silva, Flávio and others doing a CD with a mixture of singer-poets and U.S. Blues. He played two tracks, the first the story of Robert Johnson. Sebastião sings the "repentista" part accompanied by "viola;" Flávio plays the harmonica part and the third person is on slide guitar. Mike was falling asleep when I caught a taxi home to the hotel. It certainly was not a repetition of our last visit.

Back at the hotel I watched a Robin Williams movie; I was certainly not synchronized with Brazil yet; the Portuguese was an effort. I thought it was a matter of spending more time in Brazil or retiring.

Another day, events in São Paulo

I have an appointment with Plínio Martins at EDUSP at four o'clock on Friday; it will be important for me. Looking back and trying to recall the moment I think I showed him the CD of "Portrait" with the idea of translating it and becoming the future "Retrato do Brasil em Cordel."

That morning I walked up to Avenida Paulista and it took me thirty minutes to arrive at MASP (Museum of Art of São Paulo); the Brazilians say it is the best art museum in all of Latin America. The atmosphere was New York in the tropics! "I hope Keah likes the catalogue of the Museum." I returned to the hotel, took a shower and tried to rest some before tonight. It's hot so I wrote a short-sleeve dress shirt and slacks.

A bit of an irony for me: Cassia's agency is the same as the one used for the "big" musical shows in São Paulo. Last week there was one with no less than Chico Buarque de Holanda and Edu Lobo at SESC-VILA MARIANA. The critics panned it! According to Michael Grossman SESC is now the best venue for music of the major artists of Rio and São Paulo.

I called the journalist Élio Gaspari and thanked him once again for the telephone interview with me from the United States. Once again this is the Audálio Dantas connection.

The event and my talk are tonight; it will be an important moment for me and the career.

Cássia picked me up at the hotel and we had a good talk about "100 Anos." She is an aspiring actress but for the time being is doing this "gig" to make some money; she lives in Perdizes.

Photo Gallery of "100 Anos de Cordel" II

J. Borges in his market stall at the exposition

J. Borges again

Zé Lourenço, woodcut artist from Juazeiro do Norte

Curran and Abraão Batista, woodcut artist and "cordel" poet from Juazeiro do Norte

Curran and Téo Azevedo

Waldeck de Garanhuns in his market stall

J. Barros, Curran and Jerônimo Soares at the exposition

Woodcut by Jerônimo Soares at the exposition

Gonçalo Ferreira da Silva and Curran at the exposition

Azulão at the "100 Anos" Exposition

Marcelo Soares at the "100 Anos" exposition

The evening and my presentation

An Aside from my notes in English after the talk: "Well, Keah and Katie, I don't know how to say this, but it was the best!" We arrived at SESC and there was time to take photos of the entire exposition. Later there was good talk with J. Borges, Abraão Batista, Lourenço de Juazeiro, Téo Azevedo, Jota Barros and Gonçalo Ferreira da Silva, all at their poetry stands in the exposition.

Joseph Luyten once again. At that point I finally met researcher Joseph Luyten after literally years of correspondence. We wanted to have time for a long talk and to get to know each other better, but it was not possible at that moment because all the poets were present and we did not want to ignore them. Joseph and I hit it off from the start. Among other topics discussed Joseph thinks that the José Mindlin Library is the only feasible place to keep his "cordel" collection after he dies (and in fact Joseph did pass on just a few short years later and I have been in contact with his widow Sofia). Mindlin is a famous industrialist in São Paulo and is known as a bibliophile with an amazing library which is one of the few in Brazil with full air conditioning, humidity control and the rest.

Another topic: Joseph said scanning to preserve "cordel" won't work, this due to the time it takes (each page of the "folheto" in effect is a single document or file), the personnel to do it and the cost. The best is Xeroxing it, but with very high quality machines and keeping the originals intact. Joseph worked in Poitiers at the Raymund

Cantel collection of more than 9000 originals; they tried scanning and it did not turn out well.

Curran giving his presentation at the exposition

There was some confusion in that huge building that is SESC. The conference room for talks had a capacity of some 40 to 50 people and it was entirely full. All the singer-poets came and old friend Edilene Matos from Salvador as well; Joseph Luyten spoke first and like a good "paulistano" he was good – just the facts please!

My talk was for some forty to forty-five minutes, the best and best received of my entire career! There was a wonderful atmosphere of communicating with the audience, many in the room laughing heartily at the anecdotes and jokes I was telling (all this was planned and given as outlined). I thanked all for the opportunity to be there, told of my interest in "cordel" and why I began that research "odyssey" and then told many of those old anecdotes from 1966-1967. My time was up but Audálio encouraged me to go on with more stories. So I improvised a bit, most was extemporaneous, like at Brown University with Sérgio Miceli in 1994 and up to a point with Arian Suassuna at the BRASA meeting in 2000 in Recife. Basically it was the text of this talk that would become a point of departure for what would come later: "Adventures of a 'Gringo' Researcher in Brazil in the 1960s" ["Peripécias de um Pesquisador 'Gringo' no Brasil nos Anos 1960"], Trafford Publishing, 2010.

It was all recorded by "Rádio Atual". I handed out the new business cards for future contacts (with the orange cover of "A Literatura de Cordel" by J. Borges); the card listing the e-mail address and more important the new web site address of www.currancordelconnection. Regina from EDUSP showed up with copies of the new printing of "História do Brasil em Cordel" of 1998, including copies for me which I gave to Joseph Luyten, Audálio Dantas and a copy for the exposition.

Then there was a long session with photos for "Época" magazine, the best of its kind according to Audálio Dantas ("the best since 'Realidade'"). A meeting with a reporter of the same magazine is scheduled for some time tomorrow morning. There were many students and even professors wanting e-mail contact or help with theses. Not even the experience of the "50 Anos de Literatura de Jorge Amado" in 1981 in Salvador came up to this: many people surrounding me while Cássia was standing nearby with a fat envelope of cash – the honorarium. How to handle that? I managed to keep it all low key and stuff the envelope in my pocket and home to the hotel.

The most important: Audálio was duly impressed and happy; he took me to eat in an Italian restaurant afterwards and in the company of wife Vanira, a delight. I believe that honestly I contributed much to his/their happiness that day (keep in mind this is all "small potatoes" in their lives). In other words, the attendance was great, including people from the press, all as planned and desired (the success of the event will be a credit to Audálio himself and his work as "organizer-curator"). I wondered later if he had called in a few markers from old colleagues from the press; it well may be the case.

I wrote, "All this is good for the 'cordel,' but also for me and A.S.U." There was astounding publicity in São Paulo (and even Brazil) for the event. For me the experience was many times better than the talk at BRASA in Recife in 2000 and even better than "50 Years of Literature of Jorge Amado" in Salvador in 1981, and the Cuíca book moment in Salvador paled in comparison.

An aside about Audálio Dantas

Audálio was a reporter for "O Cruzeiro" in 1960 and for "Realidade" for many years (we traded stories about mutual experience in the Northeast and my trip on the sternwheeler on the São Francisco" River in 1967). Audálio had done a major, in-depth article on the river and the boats for "Realidade." He was President of the Syndicate of Journalists of São Paulo and later of the journalistic entity for all of Brazil. And it was he who first reported the story of Vladimir Herzog (imprisonment and torture and subsequent death by the military during the dictatorship), putting his own life at risk as well. He told me that he wrote the "Diary" of Carolina de Jesus, or rather, edited it for publication. He has traveled the world as a journalist and by the way knows good Spanish and French as well as his native Portuguese. At one time he did a trip by automobile from São Paulo to Mexico City; we traded stories of Guatemala, "El Lago de Atitlán," and the National Museum of History and Anthropology in Mexico City.

He was a candidate for Brazilian House of Representatives by the M.D.B. ["Movimento Democrático Brasileiro"], the "opposition" party from 1978 to 1982. He knows a lot about "cordel" and created, that is, helped organize, along with Joseph Luyten, all the festivities of "100 Anos de Cordel." Vanira is his wife and there are two daughters, 12 and 9 years old respectively. Vanira is a journalist and was a former student of Audálio's. The conversation that evening was wonderful, in a restaurant in Higienópolis.

Emotions of the Moment

I wrote, "What a difference from one year to the next! I think that all that has happened and is happening now is an excess of enthusiasm of the moment but is actually true. And there is no need to deny the "rush," – the feeling of really being appreciated for your life's work – four of my books on the presentation table during the talks and the new edition of "História do Brasil em Cordel" in the bookshops and on their computers. The new printing in 2001 is 1500 copies and Plínio Martins says there will be royalties and more printing in the future (this turned out to be accurate.)"

I gave myself some advice: "Keep breathing; keep working. The long hours, days, months and years of work all paid off tonight. (Now in 2016 while writing this I feel the same happiness but writing with a little more objectivity and distance from the event of 2001, and from Colorado and Arizona fifteen years later.) I feel really like a pioneer in research on the "cordel" and now at the height of my career. The people in Brazil in 2001 still cannot believe that I am retiring from teaching at the university and at such a 'young age.'" In 2009 when I did the first revision of these notes I asked myself: can it be that "Retrato do Brasil em Cordel" will come to pass? This was in spite of reading some of the first proofs years earlier. I wrote, "Time is passing; I don't want a posthumous work! Be that as it may, they cannot take away from me the happiness experienced in 2001."

Tomorrow will be another day; the reporters want interviews. The plan is to go to lunch with Joseph Luyten and later meet Plínio Martins at EDUSP.

All this affirms certain things: one must be persistent, honest, keep working, and good things will happen.

An Aside: It was astonishing to see how many people in attendance had read the interview in the "Folha de São Paulo," an interview done months earlier by telephone in Arizona with Élio Gaspari.

I said to myself in 2001: "You have to find a publisher for 'Retrato.' And you have to write 'Adventures of a 'Gringo' Researcher in Brazil in the 1960s' ["Peripécias de um Pesquisador 'Gringo' no Brasil nos Anos 1960"] and begin the Portuguese-English Anthology." All was done by 2009, but in 2001 I was still like Pedro Pedreiro, "Esperando, esperando, esperando o trem". I said to myself in 2001: "The good news is that this will keep you busy for two or three years. And keep in touch with Audálio; he is the key to 'Adventures' – he was enthusiastic about the talk, even "adored it," and wants more. And so it is that history repeats itself: Bahia in 1981, Bahia in 1990, Recife (a little) in 2000, and now EDUSP in 1998 and "100 Anos" in 2001. It's 3:00 a.m. and there is a big day tomorrow."

Another day: encounter with Joseph and Sofia Luyten

I slept poorly due to having drunk a strong coffee at 1:30 a.m.; no comment needed.

I awoke at 9:00 a.m. had a quick breakfast and telephoned Joseph Luyten; he lives only four blocks from my hotel, an astounding coincidence in huge São Paulo. On the walk to his place I saw many hummingbirds, one with the interesting name of "Caga Sebo" and with an all blue head. This apartment of Joseph and Sonia's is their library; there is another a short distance away where they live, that is, from Sunday to Wednesday. Their principal residence is a house on the beach in Santos where they live the rest of the week. And a house in Holland! Joseph knows six languages and goes from one to another without thinking: German, French, English, Portuguese, Spanish and now Japanese. He was born in 1941 (same as this author), arrived in Brazil in 1952 and eventually earned the doctorate at the USP in Communications. Sonia, a delightful person, also earned the Ph.D. at the USP in the "School of Communications and Arts." She is a specialist in the comics of the world, especially the "Manga" from Japan while Joseph is the same in "cordel."

Joseph told of his life: Brazil, Japan, Holland, a return to Japan, then Portiers in France and once again to Brazil. They even lived in a castle in Holland! They have three children, all girls, all adults.

They are true Latin American intellectuals with private world class libraries to match. Joseph is a bibliophile to the extreme! He is of Dutch and Irish ancestry.

His "cordel" collection is comprised of 15,000 story poems; he is one of the few persons I know who collects EDITIONS! Not just titles like me. It is difficult to add up, but he has twelve or thirteen Leando Gomes de Barros originals. He has the original books of Garnier IN PROSE including the story of Charlemagne ["Carlos Magno"] which was an important source for the beginnings of "cordel" in Brazil, a story spread from its point of origin (importation) in Rio in the south to the entire Northeast. Joseph has popular literature in verse ["literatura popular em verso"] not only from Brazil, but from Portugal, Spain, France, Italy, Chile, Peru and Argentina.

In regard to secondary sources I think he has them all. It is a huge bibliography, the definitive one. His system of cataloguing "cordel" is as follows: every entry goes by the first name of the poet and then the title of the "romance" or "folheto." Joseph hates the idea of just the title which he believes results in the anonymity of the poems and takes credit away from the poets (compare this to our own "Retrato" with just a list of titles in the bibliography, but with author, title, everything in notes in the text). I wrote, "Amazingly enough he would like to have my collection although small in comparison."

In his library there are other drawers, one with magazine articles and clips on the poets, another of all the researchers of "cordel" and his correspondence with them (he has all my letters throughout the years).

He has 1500 original woodcut blocks; they are all at present in Japan.

He is the most serious researcher (in his work) that I have ever known and by far the most METICULOUS!

He is also an art critic and has works of great value in various places.

In public he is a bit of a joker ["um brincalhão"] but was very serious with me. He is a person of great dignity and strong opinions, but in a positive sense. In 2009 when I wrote these notes he seemed to me to be one of the great intellectuals and writers of Brazil, perhaps not quite up to Câmara Cascudo in folklore but in the area of "cordel," yes.

Sônia has written books in her area of "Manga" in Japan and has her own intellectual "turf." I have the impression they will continue to research, teach and work hard to maintain their economic lifestyle indefinitely (this happened with Joseph who suffered a stroke and died a few months later after this writing of original notes in 2009). I thought to myself then in 2009 writing these notes: "I retired in 2002 but kept teaching part-time at ASU; those were good years, no regrets." By the way we enjoyed a Brazilian custom of those years of 2001, a recent novelty: food by the kilo, good, basic food, tasty and very Brazilian!

What Joseph and Sônia could bring to the United States would be the link to Japan, that is, Brazil-Japan. Joseph established Brazilian Studies in five or six places in that country.

I wrote, "These are similar things, of course in my own area that I could have done had I been allowed to establish a "Cordel Center" at ASU after my retirement. I proposed the Center shortly before 2002 but nothing came of it; the idea was not accepted by the administration." In sum, the time with Joseph and Sônia was invaluable and not to be forgotten. Joseph died some years later; Sônia sent notice and a few letters, the last time 2009.

At the University of São Paulo Press with Plínio Martins and talking about "Retrato do Brasil em Cordel"

Valdeck de Garanhuns doing a woodcut.

I took a taxi through the crazy traffic of São Paulo, the only way to get to USP on time for the meeting with Plínio. The university seemed the same as the 1996 visit, the lawns a bit overgrown, and huge. The first stop was at the university book store where I saw my "História do Brasil em Cordel;" they said the people from the "Folha de São Paulo" came by and got it today, perhaps in preparation for my interview with them tomorrow for the "Literary Supplement" of Sunday.

Upon my arrival at the press Plínio was out for lunch but seemed glad to see me upon his return. We had a good talk and he was very cordial; he is from Goiás State, Tocantins. The publishing house of "Ateliê" is a private business for him, totally apart from EDUSP. He is quite happy with results so far for "História" and believes the second printing will do well (in fact it did, a third has been done, modest sales continue as do modest royalties).

He seemed intrigued with the idea of "Portrait," the original version in English that years later would become "Retrato do Brasil em Cordel" and the CD left with him with all the illustrations - the covers of the "cordel" poems. I felt comfortable leaving it all with him; no fear of copying, plagiarism or downright theft; it was agreed I would translate "Portrait" into Portuguese by 2002.

To give the reader an idea of the publishing business in Brazil: "Ateliê" has a contract with "O Diário Oficial de São Paulo," the government press of the richest state in Brazil;

it currently has a 900 page manuscript at press on Euclides da Cunha's "Os Sertões" ["Rebellion in the Backlands"] perhaps Brazil's best known book. Plínio spoke that perhaps they would be interested in a Portuguese version of "Portrait;" I tried to sell him on the concept or thesis of the book. It was worth the risk; I would send him more details in two or three months. He said the people there could translate "Portrait" and I could read the proofs or perhaps do the text over, scanning in high resolution. I wrote: "I feel neither optimistic nor pessimisstic, but I'm glad I made the first move to do the book. I was happy to have done the book and done it well in English." (I forgot to write of the results of all this: that moment with Plínio would be the beginning of "Retrato," this in 2001 when I began to literally rewrite "Portrait" in Portuguese in Arizona and send it to Plínio in 2002, and now awaiting its publication still in 2009. They said at "Ateliê" that the final proofs will be ready in 2009, and in fact they were; I read them in 2009.)

Mission accomplished. After tomorrow all will be tourism. To prepare me for the interview with "A Folha" I am rereading "História do Brasil em Cordel."

I do not know what is going to happen with the photos already taken and the interview not yet taking place for "Revista Época'," a pity if it does not happen. I recall that the photographer did the pictures last night at SESC.

That night at the "100 Anos" exposition, interviews and encounters

I slept badly again and was feeling really worn out, perhaps due to the rereading of the long book for the interview. The next day the journalist cancelled, but I talked with her on the telephone: we spoke of Audálio, the "cordel" and the book "História."

Back to SESC and that evening; they took photos of me for the review "O Leitor," according to Audálio the best literary magazine in São Paulo. The interview should take place somewhere, somehow, sometime. (It did happen and the article turned out great; a copy is in my library in Mesa.)

I had a good talk with the poet and woodcut artist Abraão Batista at the SESC; he is one of my favorites. He was a professor of psychology before beginning "cordel" and the woodcuts. He appears in several of my books. He spoke of a trip to Florida and told many anecdotes of the experience (his Portuguese was difficult for the "gringo" to understand.) I showed him two or three pages from "História" where I had written about him and he seemed very happy about that. He has a new story-poem about the present day political scandal in Brazil (the 2001 flavor): Antônio Carlos Magalhães, Fernando Henrique Cardozo, the title: <u>WWW.Laulau.</u> If one happy day I do a revision of "História" I'll close the book with this poem. He has another on Clinton and Monica, important for "Bramundo" ("Bramundo" is the title and text of a long chapter on the outside world treated in "cordel" in Brazil which will eventually come out as one of the chapters of "Retrato do Brasil em Cordel" by Ateliê Press years later).

There was a conversation with a graduate student doing her Master's Thesis on "cordel" with some advice by yours truly.

Then came a sudden request for another interview, this for TV São Paulo in Ribeirão Preto. It was short, but well done; it came out all right.

Mark, Plínio Martins at the University of São Paulo Press

I had a good talk with Valdec de Garanhuns; he also does Puppet Theater ["Teatro de Mamulengo"] at the SESC-VILA MARIANA, but has a poetry stand and does woodcuts for "100 Anos." Many sell in Europe. An Aside: Abraão Batista quoted a price of $3000 USD for works sold in the exterior. Can this be?

There was time for a long, calm look at Joseph Luyten's exposition of story-poems for "100 Anos," a superior collection!

I felt a little uncomfortable with some of the singer-poets ["cantadores"]; they all wanted to sell me CDs. As mentioned earlier it is not my bailiwick due to a problem in hearing.

A last minute change: I had to change the airline reservation for Rio to a later time in order to appear for an interview for "TV Cultura" of São Paulo, according to Audálio "a command performance" and set up by him. I'll have to get up at 5:45 a.m., do the checkout at the hotel, do the interview and then get to the airport.

Up to this point there have been interviews with "Época," "Do Leitor," "Rádio Bandeirantes," "TV Cultura," and the "Folha de São Paulo," all good but I am paying the price – stress and a lack of sleep. I should complain! Perhaps Rio will be calmer and more relaxing.

Another day, interview with "TV Cultura" and the last moments with Audálio

Awaking at 5:45, I ate breakfast, did the checkout and was ready for Audálio at 7:30. The honorarium for SESC ["cachê"] by the way was $200 USD, a good thing because the hotel was $187.

Audálio is seventy years old in 2001; he drives like me, winding carefully through the São Paulo traffic with radio always tuned to classical music, to Higienópolis where we arrive at the gate of "TV Cultura." We spoke of politics: Vladimir Herzog was the principal reporter for this station. At the time Audálio was president of the "Diários Associados" and was the head of the journalists who denounced the torture and deaths by the military, a serious matter of the times. Herzog's story: He was "invited" to testify in the morning; by 5 p.m. he was dead a result of the torture. His death was the catalyst for many changes and protests.

I was introduced to the reporter, Miss Laila, who did a rapid perusal of the book; we spoke for five minutes and it was "on the air." There were questions about the book, how I became interested in the subject, good questions, and the changes I saw in "cordel" over the years. The interview was ten to fifteen minutes and my Portuguese held up well. Audálio summarized it all with "Good!"

Afterwards Audálio and I went for breakfast in a shiny, modern restaurant in a shopping center in Higienópolis, the newest in the city. It was our best talk of the whole time. I wrote, "This is my kind of Brazilian!" It turns out Audálio does not like "futebol," a serious sin in Brazil. An Aside: Cássia, the hostess for SESC, adores sports in the U.S.A., knows about the Phoenix Suns and has seen some of the games on TV. She explained to me the "Copa dos Libertadores," the world championship of the private professional clubs. We hit it off well.

Audálio wanted to speak Spanish with me and so it went for over an hour; his Spanish was a little rusty, but so was mine. He spoke of work trips to Peru, Chile, Argentina, Colombia, and especially to Cuba, a country he has visited three times. One anecdote in particular stands out: on one trip to Havana all the journalists were lodged together in one hotel and were notified that Fidel would be arriving to speak with them. He arrived in military uniform, a large revolver strapped to his waist. He took off the revolver, laid it on the piano, and spoke for five straight hours until 4:00 in the morning. Audálio recalled the high, almost falsetto voice of the great leader, especially when he was agitated.

My host is from the M.D.B. ["Brazilian Democratic Movement Party]; he knew Ulysses Guimarães well and even Tancredo Neves (the latter was elected president of Brazil at the end of the military dictatorship but died on the operating table the day he was to be inaugurated, "Martyr of the New Republic" ["Mártir da Nova República"]). A funny aside: Audálio says when you are on the campaign trail and have a "chance to "go," "do it!" Audálio participated in all the manifestations of the campaign for direct presidential elections ["Diretas Já"] an important chapter in Brazil's political history.

His Spanish was very correct and tended toward an Argentinian pronunciation: "cajje" and "jo." He was in Nicaragua and knew Daniel Ortega. He is pro-labor, pro-justice and a Democrat. I wrote, "I really like this man; he is one of the best Brazilians I have ever met, and that is no understatement. We really hit it off."

He speaks French and studied at the "Alliance Française." We spoke of Portugal and he has seen it all; we traded anecdotes of the language as spoken in Portugal and the contrast in Brazil.

I spoke of Mexico and the archeological zone of Palenque; he has visited the "Museo Nacional de Antropología e Historia" in D.F.

Life for him moves at an incredible velocity with no vacation time now for four years. He does a daily column for the "Diário Oficial."

He has met Jorge Amado but believes that Jorge tended to "repeat his successes." I spoke of the "50 Years of Literature of Jorge Amado" celebration in Salvador in 1980.

"Well, Keah, the interview at "TV Cultura" dealt with all these recent events and would prepare the way for the final years of the academic career as well as the productive years in retirement. I think that my guardian angel is up there taking care of me. And even if not, it all has been a great moment; I can hardly wait to tell you all about it. There was a moment when I showed Audálio all the photos I had brought with me from home; it helped to "humanize" these contacts and moments: the photos of you, Katie, Cupcake our doggy, and the trout fishing in Colorado."

Audálio spoke of his campaign for the Chamber of Deputies and the MDP party. He said it was inexpensive because he had the support of all the journalists in the country. He detests the current political corruption of 2001 and the scandals of the moment, but added that it was possible for him to leave politics without cynicism.

We later stopped by his office at "Audálio Dantas Communications." Vanira is really his secretary; she is a great person and younger than he. The phones ring fifteen hours per day and he has irons in many fires.

An Aside: "I can't believe it: the national magazine "Isto É" has an issue out with stories on Abraão Batista, Chico Buarque de Holanda and Roberto Carlos – all in their 60s! I am reliving my years in Brazil in 1966-1967." The photos "Do Leitor" took at SESC would come out later (I did not know when but it all turned up later).

Another interesting point: Audália says that his ancestors were Jews a long time ago, but now he is a "nominal" Catholic. He likes "missa lite" – a short mass of 30 minutes with no sermon. He is indeed a true humanist. The most impressive of all was the time he spent with me; I need to remember that when times are difficult (and they were at times in the future, to be told in the final chapter).

More "miscellanea" from Audálio: he smoked three packs of cigarettes per day in the political campaigning odyssey, but quit "cold" during the campaign. He spoke of the catalogue for "100 Anos" in preparation; I would receive it later, a marvelous souvenir of the moment. All this told above "cost" an extra day in São Paulo but turned out to be an invaluable memory.

Shuttle flight ["Ponte Aêrea"] to Rio

The bags are full of souvenirs of "100 Anos." (An Aside from 2009: I received an email from Sônia Luyten today with "saudades" of our times.) I traveled for the first time on TAM, Brazil's newest airline and it was great; it was like Varig in the old days: new airplanes, super clean, and cute, well-dressed stewardesses. There was a hot lunch and drink, all in a bit less than one hour of flight.

A remembered aside: My rereading of "História do Brasil em Cordel" was worth it, the book comparing "official history" with the "cordel's" version. It is possible that all the effort, meetings, etc. in recent days in São Paulo may come to nothing, but I will have fond memories of it all.

In Rio de Janeiro, events of the first days

It was a little like the old days, returning "home" to Rio: the landing at old Santos Dumont, the rush of the 737 landing on the tarmac, the loud noise of the reversing engines and "whoa!" The smell of the air hit me immediately walking down the outside staircase of the plane, the smell of the sea, the "Sugar Loaf" in the distance. There was an easy, uneventful taxi ride via the "aterro" to Copacabana and my small hotel, not as nice as the one in São Paulo, but it was okay. If you leaned way out on the tiny balcony railing you could see a bit of the beach and sea in the distance.

There was much honking of horns and many police sirens outside the hotel window at 9:30 at night, another Rio traffic jam. The next morning I went for a short walk on the mosaic "calçada" at Copacabana Beach, trying to be Brazilian, ha ha! I tried to call Roberto Froelich but he was not at home. Then I succeeded in talking to Glória Pérez from TV Globo fame and was set to see her the next day. An interesting note was she said she was free at 11:00 p.m. tonight (her normal work hour) or perhaps just the way Cariocas "do business," I said I could not make it at that hour, already exhausted from the day. We would have a wonderful encounter the next day; I would show her the CD of "Retrato" (or what was done up to that point); we would talk of her daughter Daniella and her role in "Corpo e Alma" as the young heroine Jasmine. Her office was in a luxury skyscraper near the old Fort in Copacabana between Copa and Ipanema.

So the plan that day was to have breakfast and do the walk on Copacabana in the a.m., a relief after the stress of São Paulo.

I spoke by phone with Cristina Kerti; she would be out of town, in Petrópolis for the weekend. "We spoke of Rodrigo and Letícia; there are no children yet. I spoke of our daughter doing the internship for ABC News in Chicago and of you now in Colorado. Keah, I was thinking a lot of you and wondering if you were recovered by now from Dr. Griego's treatment. There is so much to talk about but better to wait. Our motto "No News Is Good News" works; it will be great to tell all these stories in person to you in our reunion in Colorado." An aside: during the phone conversation with Cristina, I noted she was in her car on the cell phone; she was stuck in traffic and I could hear her talking to a traffic guard or policeman. News was that the restaurant had been remodeled.

A financial note: "SESC paid the 30 "reais" for my change in airline ticket to Rio; it is possible I may not even have to pay for the São Paulo-Rio stretch. We shall see; all this is due to the conversation I had with Áurea in the SESC library."

The noise from horns and sirens was deafening; it sounded like a revolution outside.

The next morning I showered, shaved, had breakfast and walked the three blocks to the Copacabana "calçada," walking or "doing Cooper" from Rua Bolívar to the port and fish market near the old fort and return. Later I swam in the miniscule swimming pool on the top of the hotel. There was an interesting conversation with Gerardo and Sônia Fontes, he now seventy years old; the two were lawyers, she a prosecuting attorney in Rio. He was originally from Piauí State and remembered the article in the old "Realidade" magazine in the 1960s: "Piaui Existe." He believed the United Nations was going to take charge of the Amazon Basin and the Pantanal in order to save them for the planet; the USA would administrate. Always something new to hear in Brazil! He said for him Arizona is symbolized by a black horse and freedom.

Fortified with a hot fudge sundae, I walked to Glória Pérez's office, 32 degrees centigrade, always in the shade and 95 per cent humidity.

Glória Pérez, author of soap operas ["telenovelas"] for TV Globo Network ["Rede Globo"]

Glória Pérez's office really combines work with small living quarters in the newest and most exclusive area of Copacabana, at the end of "Posto 6." The reader should note that she is among the top writers of soap operas ["telenovelas"] in all Brazil and works for TV Globo its largest network.

I wrote, "This is really the land of the upper crust. You must touch the buzzer outside and tell who you are and whom you would like to see and if you have an appointment. A big guard in a black suit comes, opens the door; this is security in Rio in 2001."

The "office" has a bar and a kitchenette to one side; it exudes luxury including all the computers. There is comfortable living room type furniture but mainly a bank of DVD Sony Tape Machines (to see multiple chapters of the current "telenovela" for purposes of editing and creating). Another room to the side has the office, library replete with books and photos of the family and friends. And to the side there is a small bedroom and bathroom. But above all this is a place to work! I have the impression that when Glória is in the middle of production of a new "telenovela" that she may work all night long. She said she has to do a thirty page chapter each day of production. The current "telenovela," "The Clone," now has 130 chapters (shows)!"

We watched a chapter of "Corpo e Alma," the last "telenovela" starring her daughter Daniella as the heroine Jasmine. I thought to myself: "A future project of Glória's life and work would be interesting but it never went beyond a whim."

I would love to come back to take pictures, but that may be too much to ask. What I can say is that I have never in all my stays in Brazil seen such a beautiful and impressive site – work or play! It is not necessary to say she has earned it; the stress and pressure of daily production is like nothing else in the entertainment field in Brazil.

Her daughter Daniella was a friend of Chico Buarque de Holanda in high school and knew him well. I spoke in Volume I, "Adventures," of a dating scene in Rio in 1967 when I was introduced to Chico's music.

The story of Daniella and "Cordel," my reason for being with Glória Pérez is another story perhaps to be told on another occasion. Suffice to say briefly that it is the epitome of life turning into literature and vice-versa. In the "telenovela" the young hero "galán" who falls in love with the heroine kills her in cold blood; this in effect is what happened to Daniella. In this case the "hero" had strong political and social connections in Rio, was never brought to trial, this in spite of years of effort and expensive lawyers by Glória. I do not know today in 2016 at the time of this writing if any of that ever changed. But the poets of "cordel" jumped on the story and made it famous for their readers in a plethora of story-poems of the times. It perhaps stands out as one of the great "crime" stories of "cordel."

The interview ended, the walk to the hotel was very pleasant; after a shower I returned to my hangout, "O Braseiro" where I ate like a pig: "contrafilé, farofa com ovos, molho de campanha, batata frita, arroz com legumes e duas cervejinhas."

Other moments: the Hippy Fair in Ipanema, an encounter with Roberto Froelich

The next day was difficult. I awoke at 8:00, had breakfast and took a taxi to the Hippy Fair in Ipanema; Glauco the leather artist was still there and sold me the work with the tall ship "The Cutty Sark" (my favorite, a Portuguese caravela had already been sold). It probably took thirty minutes to decide what to buy because he had such beautiful stuff; the leather "map" with the ship hangs in the office in Mesa, Arizona, yet today. Otherwise, there was little new of interest to me at the fair. There was tremendous heat and humidity yes, therefore another swim in that tiny parody of a swimming pool at the top of my modest hotel. Later I watched a film on TV and lamented the lack of contacts during this short stay; if you have contacts and friends Rio can be great. But I was okay; the problem is that this was a long four-day weekend in Rio and any contacts had left town or are busy. I did my "cooper" on the Copacabana beach walkway, swam again, bought "The Alquimist" which was a quick read and I would finish in the airport a while later.

On Monday after the long weekend there was once again an encounter with Roberto Froelich of ASU days, someone the reader has met before in this volume. He is currently working half days at an English book publisher and doing translations for large firms. He will go to Arizona on the 15th to attend old friend Doug's wedding (Doug had been a student as well in the Portuguese classes at ASU, but I knew him less well; he is a successful lawyer in Phoenix). Roberto is practicing classic guitar to play in the wedding. He continues with the avocation of "good literature." He did read my modest Spanish-Portuguese Anthology on the "Cordel" published in Spain and complimented me on it but admits that "cordel" is "not his thing." We spoke of the old days; Roberto now has been in Brazil for ten years and says he is not leaving; "It is now home."

He is really humorous; I wrote, "They broke the mold with him." He is a fanatical fan of "Vasco," plays beach soccer, lifts weights, and did Kung Fu and beach volleyball in past years. He showed much of the same spirit as our last encounter in 2000 and had no regrets for not continuing for the Ph.D. in Spanish at A.S.U. This latter endeavor he said, "É uma merda."

We went to a restaurant on Copacabana Beach where I chose "empada de siri e risotto de galinha" but could only eat one-half of the huge portion; we got a carryout ["comida para viagem"] so Roberto could enjoy it at home. We spoke in Spanish, Portuguese and English. At this point in the trip I was really fatigued and was sure my Portuguese suffered; the ex-student was correcting my Portuguese and I was glad of it! Roberto spoke much of literature and is extremely well read. More than once he said I should have stayed with him at his place during the time in Rio, but in spite of being alone a fair amount of the time I liked my independence.

"Keah, I thought a lot about you on this trip, wondering how hard it must have been to make the preparations to go up to Colorado and thinking of the new "adventure" – Katie's internship at ABC in Chicago. It would be difficult to bring you both to Brazil; our 1985 trip was perfect, the culmination!"

I only stayed with Roberto until mid-night; he would have continued the "partying," but it was okay because I slept for five solid hours, "like a log" ["em português 'como uma pedra'"]. The trip had taken a lot out of me.

On another day there was "Cooper" in the morning at the beach after breakfast in the hotel, the return and I packed my bags for the taxi to the airport: 40 "reais" but a quick ride with little traffic due to the fact it was a holiday. SESC was still taking care of me; I only discovered at check in that they paid all the airport taxes for the entire trip.

Reflecting on the trip and meditating on the future

I really liked the airport in Rio; it was clean, well-cared for and without the mobs of people at Guarulhos in São Paulo. I found my old "hangout," the little café with the decoration of all the war planes from WW II, had a sandwich, drank a beer, and read a book (waiting for the later departure).

Roberto is right: that old Brazil that I knew and that he knew initially no longer exists: "Já era." Just a pleasant aside: I never saw such tight clothing and low cut blouses on the women as this time. "Nossa!"

I was now writing these final notes during a wait of four hours in the São Paulo airport (there was the flight from Rio to São Paulo for the international flight). This airport was jammed with people, was worn and appeared dirty, but it was fun to have the time to just "hang out" and people watch. The custom at Brazilian airports of the small luggage cart (no charge) was nice, an improvement on U.S. ways. I found I was at the "bottom of the tank, running on fumes."

A Travel Aside: the Varig flight from Rio back to São Paulo was really "crappy" compared to that TAM flight days earlier from São Paulo into Rio. The total on-board service: a glass of water. The airline's excuse was that the flight was too short; this flight does continue on to Lima, Peru. Looks like things are on track for Dallas and I have empty seats in the row beside me so am hoping to sleep, thus finishing these notes now.

Professionally the trip was great; no regrets and who knows what may result from it in the future. It's like the Bible says, "A Time for All Things" ["Cada coisa tem seu lugar."]. And it is time to think about all that. It is clear that we are seeing the final phase of "cordel," or at least the "cordel" that I knew. (All would change in subsequent years: "cordel" done on the computer, printed on the printer at its side, thus avoiding the astronomical cost of the printing shops: new authors, new poetry and a new public. It would be a small "Renaissance" of the same.) The trip did give me an idea for another project: "Peripécias de um Pesquisador 'Gringo' no Brasil nos Anos 1960;" (I would do it in the first days of retirement after 2002.) And perhaps an English-Portuguese Anthology of "Cordel," but this I would do for myself and not for others – I like the challenge of translation!

An Aside: One really has to pay close attention to the announcements on the p.a. system here in the São Paulo airport; they are not nearly as clear as at Rio; you could miss a flight!

I think I have never experienced so much stress on a trip to Brazil. I was alone a lot of the time, as in the past, but simply did not have the energy or the adventurous spirit to strike out alone to do new things.

Rio was good, Saturday with Glória Pérez, Sunday at the Hippy Fair and Monday with Roberto, but there was a lot of time alone in between those encounters. What saved me were the walks on the Copa sidewalk and the swimming at the hotel pool.

What was ubiquitous were the cellphones in São Paulo and Rio and the impression that surrounded me of everyone trying to survive economically in Brazil today. It was difficult to see anything new in the culture that I had liked so much in the past.

Pondering: "In one sense everything is coming out as it should: fulfilling the retirement contract here at ASU, the program on my research here at ASU on PBS Channel 8 in Tempe, the honor at Rockhurst (The Sir Thomas More Academy for academic research for a graduate), and now the "100 Anos de Cordel" which proved so good for me. "Retrato' will be the culmination of all this."

"100 Years" was, in effect, an exposition, a cultural event. The status of "cordel," the poets, the publishers, the "old" public has gone by the way ["já era"]. The "new 'cordel'" will of course arrive in the next few years, but Brazil has evolved.

The principal question is how to deal with the retirement in 2002, trying to balance work, fun, social life and adapt to the new reality.

I wrote, "My God! Few retirees have the projects I have, the hobbies, but existing on paper is one thing, turning them into reality is quite another. Life itself. I think that everything depends on ambition, if I choose to lead a "Type A" life or not. We shall see."

The high points of the trip were seeing and being with the "cordel" poets I respect, the talk itself, meeting and being with Audálio Dantas (and Vanira) and Joseph and Sônia Luyten.

Rio, in spite of all previously written, was just "okay," I could have just as easily returned home after São Paulo. As I said, the problem was the long four-day weekend, knowing few people in Rio and new things to do in Rio. (I think I have a new perspective now in 2016, rewriting these notes, but this was what I thought in 2001.)

I wrote to Keah, "Okay babe. I look forward to sitting on the porch at the cabin and telling you all about this. And talking of our adventures in the years to come. All my love, May 1, 2001."

And now as I write this, fifteen years later, it all turned out as we had hoped: good years, many new things and most good.

End. Brazil, 2001

CHAPTER VIII

BRAZIL 2002

The Motive - Taking the manuscript and materials of "Retrato do Brasil em Cordel" to Plínio Martins at "Ateliê" in São Paulo and reading an academic paper at the USP. It will be the last academic trip to Brazil before retirement in 2002.

The departure, the flight, arriving in Rio and later in São Paulo

There was "super shuttle" to the airport in Phoenix and then came a storm in Dallas which delayed our departure for one hour. We left Phoenix at 3:00 p.m. with a good flight, good connections in Dallas with the international flight only about 1/3 full to capacity. The dinner was salmon; I slept only about three hours and arrived, as usual, exhausted in São Paulo.

I caught a taxi downtown to the city center for 40 "reais," to a hotel in the Jardins District, pretty but noisy. I tried to take a nap but could not. I called Plínio Martins and set up an appointment for one p.m. the next afternoon.

The first night, the opening of the conference

I caught a bus to the conference opening at the USP and had to remind myself that it was the talk that would pay for most of the expenses for this trip, but in my mind was certainly not the main motive. The talks that night were really long and boring. Afterwards there was a "coquetel" with hundreds of students and conference participants; the former come for the free drinks and eats. I met a professor from Berkeley, another from London but the most interesting was Lourdes from México who was a specialist on documentary films about trains. She was originally from Barcelona and is one of the "invited guests," not me this time around! How things have changed from "100 Anos de Cordel" just one year ago, but that was the "jeito," the paper paid for the trip. Afterwards there was a beer in the bar at the hotel with folks from the conference and to bed; I was exhausted!

Surprise! I have a roommate, a movie director from Salvador da Bahia, one Antônio Olavo; he brings a new documentary film on Canudos (more on this later). It was a small shock in terms of privacy, actually the first time I had to share a hotel room at a conference, and with a stranger. However, it turned out well; Antônio Olavo once again "opened" the world of Canudos to me (I had read and studied "Os Sertões" ["Rebellion in the Backlands"] years earlier.

Another day, the conference

I woke hungry for breakfast and then a bus to the conference. My initial session was small, on "Oral History" with few people in attendance; so be it. In general it was pleasant; I spoke for some ten minutes on the "literatura de cordel" and "História do Brasil em Cordel" and the latter's relation to oral history (almost none). I repeated some of the talk on "Peripécias" at "100 Anos" of 2001. It still seems so strange to me to travel 4000 miles to give a ten minute talk! Such are the workings of the academic world.

Lunch that day was a bit of an experience: it was in a simple cafeteria of the USP with a librarian from the suburbs of São Paulo. The menu that day was "feijoada," black bean stew, the national meal in much of Brazil; I ate only the rice and beans fearing the rest, the "unknown tripas" (the reader may recall the fragile stomach of this "gringo"). It was little food but did the trick. I could not bear any more of the conference that day and "split the scene." One should recall that in just a few short months I was going to retire from full-time teaching at the university and after so many years in that endeavor, sitting down to listen to academic talks of no interest to me was indeed not a priority on this trip. (I was just a "good boy" all those previous years, attending meetings and talks often of little interest, but fulfilling my obligations). The discipline of spending eight hours a day on campus, five days a week, for 34 years was different; I loved my job of teaching.

I took a taxi to the hotel and called Audálio Dantas; I will see them all tonight or this coming weekend. I am so happy to have them; I know so few people here. My stomach is in revolution; that should be no surprise after the cafeteria "feijoada;" tonight I had chicken soup, room service.

The best news: Mark at the University of São Paulo Press with Plínio Martins

The next day I was with Plínio Martins at the University of São Paulo Press and he was extremely gracious to me. I delivered all the materials for the new publication (and eventually my best in Brazil): the CD with "Retrato," samples of "folhetos," photos, all for the illustrations in the book, all excellent in the final version. My organization of it all turned out to be beneficial. Plinio says he "adores" the theme of "Retrato" and will be a really fine book, one "better" than "História do Brasil em Cordel" by the USP Press in 1998 and 2001. He spoke in passing of a 900 page book just completed at "Ateliê," an edited version of "Os Sertões." He says Ateliê is recognized as one of four fine publishers in Brazil. He plans to start the revision of my text right away, "the easy part." The plan is to do it with an "agreement" ["convênio"] with the "Imprensa Oficial," a book for collectors of books and libraries with good illustrations and much art.

I wrote, "If it comes out as planned, it will be the culmination of a career's work." For the publication party, Plínio plans to do a reprinting of some famous story-poems at the same time as the book and to use them as marketing. He teaches a graduate class in publishing and the students will do the "folhetos." He added he did a similar thing for the "Bienal" and the story-poems sold like hotcakes, each for "1 real," a great advertising gimmick.

All his ideas sound good; he estimates there are now close to 200 books waiting between EDUSP and Ateliê, but that my book might be ready as soon as the end of 2002 or early 2003. It should not be a surprise that mine came out only years later but was a really fine product by Ateliê.

Another day, miscellaneous moments at the conference

I dragged myself out of bed late at 8:30 a.m., showered, shaved, had a quick "cafezinho" and caught a bus to the conference at USP. It was pleasant enough in the morning and I spent time revising my notes for the round table discussion later in the day.

A tourist note: the breakfast at the hotel was the normal and good - fruit juices, pineapple, eggs with bacon and "café com leite." The lunch the day of the talk was indeed more plentiful: I went with the group to a "churrascaria" my favorite type of restaurant in Brazil. It was a great experience in terms of food: "Camarão com alho, uma variedade de saladas e legumes, pedaços ótimos de carne – da picanha, o corte melhor." There was good conversation with Luís, a medical psychiatrist from Bahia who accompanies his wife to the conferences. He was born in the 1930s and recalls seeing the poet Cuíca de Santo Amaro on the streets of the city, but saw Rodolfo Coelho Cavalcante a lot more. He spoke of the head of Lampião in the Nina Rodrigues Museum: "A Trophy." (One recalls he is both M.D. and a psychiatrist.) His wife Elisete is a specialist in pre-historic archeology. She "adores" the Anazasi in our southwest and the "Museo Nacional de Antropología e Historia" in Mexico City.

The bad news: we arrived one hour late to the conference because of a foul-up with the credit cards and the usual Brazilian bureaucracy. The session had gone on for twenty minutes, but it turned out fine. The scene this time was different from 2001: we speakers at the long table in front and a full auditorium of perhaps 200 people. My part came out well, extremely well; there were compliments from the chair of the session ["chefe da mesa"] on all my past work in Brazil; I daresay he had done his homework. I did reasonably well speaking of Olavo's film on Canudos.

I wrote, "I am totally happy with this my last official talk representing ASU. One more time: I am retiring 'at the top of my game.'" There was humor and I did a good job of public relations for Olavo's film. There were two professors from Germany, two from Brazil and I who filled out the session.

Later: I caught a taxi for $7 USD to the hotel, a relief to not have to try to deal with the bus system. Sample news on the TV: Three thieves have just killed three passengers on a bus in Campinas; there is a gunfight on the streets of Rio outside the tunnel to Laranjeiras; and the police are battling drug kings in the "favelas" of Rio. Stray bullets hit a child in a pre-school nearby. Perhaps the reader may understand why I hesitate to spend more time here with such things going on. There was an article in the national news magazine "Veja:" "Places where "cariocas" can no longer go."

Dinner with the Dantas family

My hosts were Audálio, Vanira, the two daughters Juliana and Mariana, and Vanira's mother Dona Olga. The menu for the evening was terrific for my tastes: great conversation, a cocktail, and a meal of delicious "picanha," rice, another meat, wine from the São Francisco Region of Brazil (Audálio must have remembered our conversations of the sternwheelers and the river), and "flan." I think I asked for seconds.

Reminiscences from the conversation: Audálio is currently president of the Uylsses Guimarães Association in São Paulo (Guimarães was vice-president of the "Câmara de Deputados" in Brasília when Audálio was in the national congress). O Globo purchased the newspaper where Audálio did columns, "O Popular" and Audálio voluntarily resigned. He still works with his own consulting company: All.com.

He showed photos of his most recent trip: to Iraq and Bagdad and Babilônia. His politics are on the left so he is opposed to official U.S. policy there like almost all the Brazilians. History certainly bore him out! We listened to great music during the evening: Bach, the "Quinteto Armorial" and St. John's Passion (I think I mentioned he listens only to classical music during the commutes in São Paulo).

Back at the hotel there was finally time to have a good talk with Antônio Olavo. He is from very modest roots, poor in fact, does not have a university degree, and earns a living making short, documentary films. He is from the extreme left in politics (I noted he would be in good company with daughter Katie). The film over Canudos has opened many doors for him in Brazil, but in spite of it all, life is very precarious economically. I gave him what leads I could to contact "Brazilianists" to distribute the film. He also does spectacular calendars (with his art photos) to sell as a sideline.

The difficult decision of leaving the conference and Brazil early

For the first time I slept well on this trip, six or seven hours perhaps; I ate so much the preceding day that I was now with little appetite. For the first time in all my trips to

Brazil since 1966 I made the decision to cut the trip short and return home early. "I will be leaving tonight at 10:00 for Dallas and then home." I would be retiring later this year from ASU. Here was my rationale:

All was accomplished in São Paulo at the conference and at EDUSP with Plínio Martins.

I saw Audálio and his family.

If I do not leave now I will have two "dead" days on the weekend in São Paulo with no company.

I have no desire to do tourism alone.

I would have six days in Rio with only two social contacts planned. The only loss would be not seeing Roberto Froelich.

So there is no social motive for Rio and no other social contact; I would be alone for five days!

I did this in 2001 and do not want to repeat it.

The financial part: I will not have to pay for the flight change (cancelled now) to Rio.

They did not charge the $100 penalty for the ticket change. I would have spent more than that if I had gone to Rio; the hotel in São Paulo was paid by the conference talk.

I wrote to Keah, "My piece of mind and yours has no price. I will be back in Phoenix one week early and will still have several days to settle matters at ASU and close my office. There will be time to practice and prepare for the Colorado music "gig" – Christina's Restaurant."

It is evident rewriting the original notes for the first time now in 2009 that I really rationalized the decision to leave Brazil early. There are those who may say it was a dumb decision, but my "emotional and mental space" was what it was! I already noted my reasons.

Last days in São Paulo, notes on the trip

I spoke with Antônio in the hotel and we said goodbye. Near the hotel on another corner was a fine northeastern folk art store. I had time to look at their stock – among other things clay dolls from Caruaru and woodcuts from J. Borges. I gave them my name and the title of the book at USP. The firm has been operating for eighty years in São Paulo; they seemed to actually appreciate my hints on northeastern art, "cordel," etc. The daughter goes to Pernambuco to buy merchandise; there were many paintings I would like to have at home.

I made my last telephone call to Audálio to say goodbye (an aside: a call to a cell phone from the hotel costs $5 USD!). It was Corpus Cristi Day with 100,000 people in the plaza of the Metropolitan Cathedral and Cardinal Arns celebrating the mass.

I caught a taxi to Guarulhos, $24 USD with little traffic considering it was São Paulo. It took 25 minutes to do the check – in; they wanted to charge $100 USD for the change in the ticket, but when I told of the reasons for the change, they dropped the charge (try that today in the US). There was a three hour wait for the international flight, so I bought a Luís Fernando Veríssimo book and read it while waiting. (I am writing these notes in the waiting room of the airport eating cashews and drinking a beer; I can feel I am beginning to relax, and it is not due to the beer. I will be in Mesa tomorrow and will call you in Colorado; let's see if I can find some "doce de coco" or "chocolate" presents. Your retirement present for me, the travel bag from Beans, served me well, that is, as long as I could keep track of all its compartments."

I saw no Hedra books at the airport; they are on the computer but not on the shelves (the series was a success in 2009). My book "História" yes is in the USP bookstore.

A Brazilian Aside: in the bar Lorena at the hotel there was a young guy singing, many songs from the U.S. but in Portuguese, and a lot from MPB from the 1960s which I recognized. An opinion: I think I lived in Brazil in the best era of popular music and popular culture. There is so much to be grateful for – my new "career" in music coming up in Colorado.

A Tourist Aside: Clothing in São Paulo. A jacket, many in leather, for the "cold" weather of the São Paulo winter. My green chamois shirt-jacket saved the day for me on cold days; but there were as many hot days in a short sleeved shirt.

My Portuguese gradually improved in the days in the city. But it depended totally on the atmosphere: if there was background noise in the area or even the diction of the person who was speaking. The compliments on my Portuguese during the round table discussion with the 200 people in the audience were incredible.

The women and dress: I did not see as many beautiful women as in Rio, or the tight and low cut clothing; in part it is the climate but also I think São Paulo is just different than "tropical Rio."

Notes in the airport, thinking about the future

The most important question is the FUTURE. I recognize my temerity in dealing with Brazil at this point in the career and my life. It is very complicated but is probably due to the changes in Brazil in this the final phase of the "cordel" research in Brazil and the difficulties in adapting to this situation. I recognize all this could be seen as a lack of flexibility to search out new adventures in life on my part, but it is what it is. I find myself thinking more of "home" in Arizona. Maybe I'm finally turning into an "office researcher" ["pesquisador de gabinete"] that phenomenon so disliked by mentor Câmara Cascudo in Natal in 1966, something I've never been but may be now.

I find myself thinking of my "excuse" to leave São Paulo early, of my offer to do music in Colorado, the "new career" and necessity to prepare for it.

The unknown will be the projects during retirement; I'm feeling better thinking of it, just "meditating" here and now in the airport. The ideas for new projects, the funding for trips, the means to publish books in the future – for the meantime they are all "tabled" ["estão na gaveta"].

I think with time the enthusiasm for Brazil will return; the big hobbies will be the "memory books – the snapshots," like the project "The Farm" (the book about growing up in Kansas). An Aside: in fact it came to fruition, in fact I have to do a count; there are perhaps ten volumes of memories by Trafford Publishing, all of them based on travel diaries during forty years of work, teaching and travel. And my site on the internet: currancordelconnection.com.

It just "hit me between the eyes – the so specialized world of the research, the writings in Brazil, the interests of the reading public in Brazil and my books in Brazil, this even in spite of what the Brazilian professors told me of the good reputation all this has in Brazil. There is very little real interest in "cordel," thus my work. Plínio Martins and others think differently; I have to "keep the faith" and believe in their vision. "Retrato" will be the culmination if it comes out (and it did years later).

The future is Arizona and Colorado and the retirement. I am ready to begin the summer activities such as fishing and hiking to see flowers in high meadows, "Music in the Mountains" and its classical festival and what may come of the summer school at Fort Lewis College in Durango. The latter was a program of interesting courses for retirees where I taught; unfortunately it lasted for only one year. But I would go on to teach part – time: one course in advanced Spanish culture during the spring term only at ASU from 2002 to 2011.

I wrote, "Let's see how it all evolves. It won't be easy, a challenge for the future. Priority number one is our life: you, me and Katie."

That ended all the ruminations, returning home in 2002 and the incipient retirement.

Time would pass until 2005 and my first return to Brazil during retirement, then with another perspective, I'll tell it all in the next and final chapter.

Chapter IX

BRAZIL 2005

The Motive: Dealing with the manuscript of "Retrato do Brasil em Cordel" in São Paulo, tourism and a final conference in João Pessoa

The flight and the arrival in São Paulo

I caught the Super Shuttle to the airport in Phoenix, arrived well, but there was a two hour delay in the flight to Dallas where upon arrival I caught the "sky train" to the international terminal. The American flight from Dallas: the new thing was that now one had to pay for a scotch drink; the "free drink" on international flights was over. The food was minimal but just "okay." I slept little or none feeling terrible upon arriving in São Paulo.

View from the Century Plaza Hotel

The arrival in São Paulo: there was a long line at customs but no major problems. I caught an airport bus to the downtown center and from the stop it was a short walk to the hotel. The hotel itself was fine and in a good neighborhood but I felt lost – the labyrinth of São Paulo!

I telephoned Audálio Dantas and it was good to talk again to my friend. I also made an appointment at EDUSP to talk with Plínio Martins and text editor Marilene about revisions for "Retrato."

Interview on "TV São Paulo"

The first surprise was Audálio had set up an interview for me on "TV São Paulo" for that first afternoon. He picked me up and we went directly to the TV station in an impressive skyscraper on Avenida Paulista, the "5th Avenue" of the city, the building also the headquarters for the city legislature. It is like PBS in the U.S., an intellectual program about literature.

The host is Levi Ferrari, a true veteran and master of his medium; during the twenty minute interview we talked of "História do Brasil em Cordel," of "cordel" itself and of Brazilian Literature (a good thing my background was solid in the latter, I could speak of Mário de Andrade and João Guimarães Rosa and not just of Jorge Amado). All was videotaped for showing later; the channel is for the intellectual elite, a very small public. Vanira said she would make a copy for me, but it never came to pass. Afterwards Levi invited us across the street to his favorite "cafezinho" place. I almost, almost felt part of the atmosphere of greater São Paulo: "Avenida Paulista," "TV São Paulo," and a social moment with the "literati." There was another compliment from Audálio: the book is free of literary jargon and is really a contribution in the area. He continues as one of the "stars" of the journalistic and literary scene in São Paulo, this aside from his TV presence.

I invited Audálio, Vanira, Juliana and Mariana to Sunday lunch.

Audália Dantas reviewing questions from Katie Curran for the MST

Afterwards we went to Audálio's office where he sat at the computer and "fixed up" Katie's questions for the management of MST interview. Audálio helped me arrange a videographer for the whole thing for $50 USD.

Back to the hotel that night at 9 p.m.; I was exhausted. Room service of a filet and a couple of beers. Diary notes: I tried to telephone the Luytens but no luck; they must be in Santos.

Curran does tourism in São Paulo

I slept a little; I felt a little better and there was a good breakfast. I took a deep breath and walked up to Avenida Paulista where I caught the subway to the "Praça da Sé" and the "Catedral Metropolitano." The church was jammed with people; the occasion is a local custom: the crowning of saints for all the districts of São Paulo; afterwards the image of the saint can be taken to each parish.

Mark outside the "Catedral Metropolitana"

"Pátio dos Jesuitas," São Paulo

The "Praça da Sé" – popular life in São Paulo: it was a little like the plazas in northeastern Brazil of years ago, but a little "folkloric" and frightening.

An Aside: There is something different; my hotel is astonishingly quiet at 11:00 p.m. This is totally out of the ordinary for past experiences in Brasil.

I return to the "Pátio dos Jesuítas," the college founded by the Jesuits in São Paulo in 1554! There was a relic: the bones of Father José de Anchieta. I saw the church, the museum and ate lunch in the restaurant. It was extremely pleasant: fresh air, clean air with a lot of sunshine.

An Aside: the Subway. There were fewer people on Saturday; I was on many lines with many changes, but it was all clean, a good system and experience. A memory: it was far different from the old age and dirtiness of the subway in Madrid in the late 1980s.

The ceramic bull and child outside the Museum of Art of São Paulo

I decided to return to the Museum of Art of São Paulo, one of the best of all Latin America. It was good; not only is it the best in all Brazil, but there was a traveling exposition of Expressionism, one hundred works of the masters. My wife Keah would know them all; my favorite is Renoir. I had a good lunch in the Museum and took the subway home, now very tired.

Assis Ângelo at home

Assis Ângelo at home

Assis Ângelo and his northeastern clay doll collection

I called Assis Ângelo, not only the master of northeastern culture in São Paulo, but also "cultura popular" and journalism" (a "guru" in São Paulo told me all this). Miraculously he was home and free, and so after many subway changes I arrived at his apartment – a true museum of Northeastern Art. We spoke of "TV Internet" of São Paulo where he has a program each week. Afterwards we repaired to a very noisy "pé sujo" where over draft beer we spoke of everything, i.e. politics in Brazil included. He gifted me with a book called "Cordel no Metrô," CDs and DVDs. Afterwards, exhausted, I caught the subway "home" to the hotel where I settled for room service, a great sandwich and two small beers. Luckily I was able to catch a documentary on TV of much interest: "The Jesuits in the South of Brazil."

At the folk art fair of the State of São Paulo

There was a treat for me that next day. Audálio picked me up at noon; on a Sunday the city and transit are relatively calm. We stopped by his house where I met Vanira's mother and the two daughters, Juliana and Mariana. I had to retell the story of the bear at the cabin in Colorado one more time to Mariana; she had written a story in school about it. Juliana is as they say in Brazil "um broto," a budding teenager; she will take the "vestibular" or entrance exams for the university this Fall.

Photo Gallery of the outing in "Parque Água Branca" and the Folk Art Fair

Audálio, Vanira and Mariana at the Folk Art Fair of the State of São Paulo

Audálio tasting a local "cachaça" at the fair

Bolivian Dancers at the fair

Audálio in the "forest" at the park

The Dantas took me for a fine and unexpected outing to the "Parque Água Branca" with its bamboo, old trees and a stream, all unexpected in this metropolis, all beginning with an "água de coco." This fair takes place once a year in the entire State and was highly "civilized" compared to the norm of northeastern fairs I frequented previously. The Fair's motto is "Revealing São Paulo." There were arts and crafts from every "county" or "município" of the State; it was highly organized, clean and with fine arts and crafts. I took photos of the woodworking: birds, fish and trains! There were beautiful regional folkloric dances on the sound stage where I saw surprisingly enough in all their regalia Bolivians, Paraguayans, and local German and Russian dancers from the State. I did conclude that the Northeast is not the only place in Brazil with good folk art!

Afterwards we had a fine lunch at a place near famous Paecambu Soccer Stadium (Carlos Prestes gave his famous "return to Brazil after exile" speech there in 1945) in the open air under the trees and with a very calm atmosphere. It employed that Brazilian quirk: food by the "kilo" and was tasty: salmon filet, rice and beans and a cold beer. There was a gratuitous "aperitivo," one of my favorites in Brazil: "batida de coco" and "batida de maracujá" as well. And great coffee. I was relaxed and could tell jokes – no stress! That would come the next day with a long subway ride, then a taxi connection to the headquarters of the "Movement of Those without Land" [MST] and then a hurried trip to the São Paulo University Press [EDUSP].

Today the city of São Paulo seemed like a good place to live: calm, little pollution or traffic and good weather. I had not experienced much of that prior to that day; I forgot to say that the Fair was in the District of Higienópolis.

Audálio dropped me off at the hotel at 5:00 p.m.; I rested for a while and then walked five long, uphill blocks to Avenida Paulista to a large and modern shopping center. The movies did not appeal to me, so I did a very unlikely thing for Curran: window shopping and the walk home.

So it was a good weekend in São Paulo, something I had not experienced before (writing now, it shows that anywhere can be pleasant if you are in good company).

Audálio passed on a good travel "clue" ["jeito"] for São Paulo: the way to get to far off Guarulhos Airport – take a taxi to the "city" airport of Congonhas and there is a free bus to Guarulhos, with the proviso you don't have to be in a hurry.

The next day turned out as I had hoped; I got up at 7:15, showered and had breakfast, preparing myself for come what may with the MST. Gustavo the MST secretary phoned at 10:00 a.m. telling me that the chief Gilmar Mauro was busy and they would get back to me later in the p.m. with an update. Audálio explained that this is like the rest of Brazil; the MST is not lacking in bureaucracy.

With Plínio Martins at the University Press of São Paulo

Another surprise ["imprevisto"] – there was an unexpected call from Marilene, Plínio's assistant at the press. USP has just gone on strike; they all had to clear out of the EDUSP building and are now temporarily at the College of Arts and Communications. "Can you come now?" I said "Of course" and hopped the metro to Vila Madalena and a taxi to USP. There would be all kinds of student meetings regarding the strike.

Plínio as always was very pleasant and seemed pleased to see me once again. Much of the time he was busy on the telephone so I had a chance to chat with his "second in charge" Marilene. Married with one child, she is originally from Santa Catarina (blond and pretty) with a degree from USP in 1992. She has worked at EDUSP for five years and is now in Plínio's office, "second in command"'. She read and corrected the "Retrato" manuscript and is now up to the 5th chapter (one-half done); there were lots of corrections and she had some "questions." Uh oh. The agreement is for me to take the first five chapters home, read, make comments and return to her by e-mail. She said my Portuguese was good, but oftentimes "We don't say it that way." However, good news, to this point there are no re-writes. (This is sounding much like the often agonizing publishing odyssey in the U.S.) It turned out she indeed did not have my latest version of the book with all the notes, a good thing I had brought the "back up" with me on CD. She was pleasant enough but not too encouraging: there are many projects at the press, a lot of work to be done, and she only hopes to finish the revision by 2005 (we are in 2002)! It was a good conversation with lots of humor; I took photos of her, Plínio and myself.

I took Plínio to lunch and we had a good conversation: we spoke of the USA, of the War in Iraq, the hurricane going on in the U.S. and Brazilian corruption. Note: Plínio does not like the MST and says they are living on handouts from the government, by now up to 40 million "reais." (I was gradually learning that the MST is truly controversial in Brazil and far from the majority approve of it.)

Also eye-opening were details of the publishing business in Brazil in 2002. There are currently 200 manuscripts at the EDUSP to read and revise and 100 at Ateliê! Printing in Brazil is an "atrocity;" you have only ninety days to make full payment. I wrote later, "I shall not hold my breath on this one." It is ironic to see all this later in 2005. In spite of all this he really likes the book and sees it as an "album" joining text and art. He has all the "folhetos" in hand and will scan them into the book (this was done in the proofs that I only would see much later in September and October of 2009). He is still planning on a "pretty" book. Almost in passing, I reminded him of my promised subsidy in dollars; he had actually forgotten about it and did not remember either the amount or when it was due. I said, "At the autograph party!" He wants cash; a check is complicated and "does not cut it" ["não dá!"].

Back at the hotel I was tired as usual from it all and spent time re-packing bags for the rest of the trip. I said, "There is no way to guess what will happen in the coming days, but tomorrow I have to catch the plane to Rio where I hope to get rested up."

Interview with Gilmar Mauro of the MST

I caught the metro to Barra Funda and then walked six to eight blocks to the MST Offices in São Paulo where I interviewed Gilmar Mauro, member of the national council of MST. The interview turned out fine, along with a very professional video done by a videographer arranged by Audálio Dantas (I learned later that the cameraman Roberto had never finished college and lamented the abysmal possibilities for college graduates in Brazil – "There are no jobs.")

The interview was very good as I said and "If I get it home to Katie, it will be one of the best for her film 'Greening the Revolution' which treats subsistence agriculture in a capitalist world. The film will go on to be shown today in 2016, available on U-Tube and her Facebook page."

Some details on Gilmar's life: he was only able to finish the eighth grade because at that time the family was "dispossessed" of their land and all moved to an MST Encampment. He talks like a politician (this is another matter), but in the interview he went far beyond my expectations – he had answers to ALL the questions. The logging of the interview later on was a long, laborious process, but as they say, "The pleasure was mine." See Katie's film where he does appear briefly.

Departure from São Paulo and the flight to Rio

There was a light breakfast in the hotel; Audálio was busy so I caught a taxi to the Congonhas Airport and the TAM's airport bus on to Guarulhos, a question of 45 minutes; all this was followed by the bureaucracy of paying the airport taxes. TAM makes American Airlines appear third-class; there was a very quick flight to Santos Dumont but with a tasty lunch of hot pizza and time for a beer, all this in normal tourist class.

In Rio I caught the "Real" Bus," (a "frescão" in pretty bad shape) and we went through heavy rain in downtown Rio; I got off in heavy rain with my heavy bag at Santa Teresa Street and walked to the hotel. It was quite a change from the hotel in São Paulo, but the price was right; there was no room service but you could call out for a pizza. The room was small and the area noisy. I thought in retrospect, "São Paulo was fine, I accomplished what I wanted to do, and the social life with the Dantas was great. The only problem: there is no ocean or beach."

At the Casa de Rui Barbosa Foundation and an encounter with Raquel Valença

Two blocks from the hotel there is a bus stop to the Metrô and then a ten block ride on the Metrô to old, familiar Rua São Clemente and a reasonable walk to the Casa de Rui. There was rain and an umbrella was in order.

Changes at the Casa de Rui: I was at the Research Center with the director Raquel Valença (she said that she was the one who "corrected" and edited my text on "cordel" and "Grande Sertão: Veredas," the 1985 study that won the Orígenes Lessa Prize.) We talked of the "old times:" Thiers Martins Moreira, Homero Senna, Maximiano Campos, Sebastião Nunes Batista and Adriano da Gama Kury (he now is eighty-one years old and suffered a heart attack eight years ago). I thought, "The Casa de Rui is now a cemetery; everyone I knew is either all gone or deceased."

Raquel spoke of the possibility of my giving a "short course," ten days in Paraíba and ten days at the Casa de Rui. Ha ha. I consulted the "cordel" library and found little new. And I found my book "A Presença de Rodolfo Coelho Cavalcante na Moderna Literatura de Cordel" gathering dust and mildewing in the basement of the Casa de Rui; it was and still is the worst case of distribution of my books in Brazil!

Photo Gallery of the encounter with former student Roberto Froelich

Mark and Roberto Froelich at the "pé sujo" bar and "choppe" beer in Rio

Mark on Copacabana Beach

A complete view of Copacabana

The famous mosaic sidewalk of Copacabana

That afternoon after an "almoço pelo kilo," I returned to Copacabana and went to the Othon Hotel to my old "hangout," the lounge on the third floor, calm and quiet with a beautiful view of the sea and awaited the arrival of Roberto. We chatted for half an hour and repaired to a "pé sujo" for beer, an excellent conversation and then a dinner of "galeto, molho e arroz à campanha," but without the customary beers of past visits.

Roberto is now a "Kardecista" Spiritist and a bit involved with "Umbanda," he explained all the details (Orígenes Lessa, speaking from experience, warned me years earlier of the dangers of the latter). Roberto has a vast reading in Brazilian Literature. He spoke of the old days at ASU, of friends Darío and Douglas, the latter now a millionaire in real estate development in Phoenix. Roberto lives from month to month doing translations and giving classes for executives in English. He left the study of the classical guitar (and he had concert capabilities), giving the instrument to a friend (intimating it was a counsel from "Umbanda.") He says now the MST is just another political entity in Brazil, and most Brazilians do not like it, a result of its dependence on government handouts. He says that poverty and violence in Rio "now" are incredible, and he has seen them worsen in his sixteen years in Brazil. He does voluntary work in Jacarepaguá, a trip of one hour and a half by bus from his apartment. Friend Doug offered to buy him an apartment in Rio, but he prefers now to live in Chapéu da Mangueira, a "favela" [slum]. He often hears the noise of gunfire at night; the drug traffickers know him but leave him alone, calling him "Professor." He would like to be a university professor but can't stand the "rigmarole" of literary criticism today or the "bagunça" in the universities. He gives books to the poor people living in the "favela," yet has taught classes on "Grande Sertão: Veredas" to wealthy private students.

View from the hotel in Rio

It turns out there is a "favela" immediately behind my hotel in Rio and the tunnel of "Rua Barata Ribeiro" is a bit beyond that. I can see the "movimento" from my hotel room at night and all the drinking going on in the streets. I did tourism with Roberto today: bus and subway to Cinelândia downtown, the bar "O Amarelinho" in front of the Municipal Theater, the National Library and the National History Museum. We drank "Guaraná," Roberto spoke of Spiritism and gave me a copy of Kardec's "Book of the Spirits." We walked through downtown and ended up at the FUNARTE [National Foundation of the Arts] bookstore where I purchased sixteen "folhetos" of the "cordel" poet Gonçalo Ferreira da Silva (recall the "Casa de São Saruê" in Santa Teresa) and the "cordel" book by Hedra Publishing on João Martins de Atayde.

There was a good lunch of "galeto, molho à campanha, batata frita, arroz e choppe." We then walked to Praça 15 and took the old ferry boat to Niterói; there was a long walk to the "Mercado São José" and its fish market where we saw octopus, squid, sardines, salmon from Chile, shrimp and more than twenty kinds of fish. Then came the ferry back to Rio, Copacabana Beach, a beautiful day, some beer and huge waves along the beach ["a ressaca"].

By now I was more than a little tired maybe due to a lack of a nap and there was a cold coming on. I had now been in Brazil for more than one week. That evening we went to a café with "churrasco pelo kilo, canja de vinho, picanha, e arroz" (the price: $ USD 5). A money exchange note of the times: I had changed money, at first 2.25 reais to the dollar; later it was 1.7 reais to the dollar and my money was worth a lot less; I made a note to remind myself of this for the next trip.

So up to now I have not felt the usual loneliness, but the traffic, the effort to speak Portuguese, the pollution and the crowds of people have affected me. Our life in Arizona and Colorado is easy by comparison! In spite of everything Roberto saved the day in Rio!

Last Day in Rio

I found São Paulo much less noisy, polluted and full of people than Rio, but then there is the sea and the beach!

After breakfast I returned the "folhetos" on Daniella Pérez to the reception desk at Glória's place and then took advantage of the moment to walk on the Copacabana "calçada" from one end to another, seeing the fish market near the fort. I packed bags once again and then was once more with Roberto at the "Sindicato do Choppe," then dinner at my spot "O Braseiro" (there was at this writing in Mesa, Arizona, an overview of the Olympics and Rio in 2016 and they featured "O Braseiro!"), and then to a "pé sujo" until 9:30 p.m. Roberto wanted to continue the partying and talk again of old times; he spoke of the debt he owes me in the classes and then said something strange: "You won't be seeing me again." In fact this happened; the only news I received later was that he moved out of Rio and was living on a small farm. I have no contact information and wonder if we will cross paths again. That was an emotional moment for both of us, ole' professor and favorite student. There was a goodbye, my return to the hotel and turning in at midnight.

The departure from Rio and "suffering" in Salvador

There was a quick taxi ride to the Galeão Airport with no surprises; the airport seemed antiseptic after the city. After arriving in Salvador I took the "frescão" to the city along the still beautiful green-blue sea and arrived at my hotel.

Mark "suffering" at the hotel in Salvador

For this final trip I had made a reservation via internet at the hotel which is on the hill "O Corredor da Vitória," one of my favorite parts of the city. There was a beautiful view of the sea way down below, but my room was on a high floor facing the street, plus hammering next door (they must have been remodeling some rooms). I succeeded in changing rooms the next day; the new room was on the other side, very high up, with a view of the pool down below and the ocean beyond. There was a little "cog train" from the pool down the steep incline to yet another pool with a bar. The blue-green water below was inviting but I was told it is seven to eight meters deep and I was not ready to take on that challenge. Instead I chose to swim in the pool above outside the lobby and then had a light lunch; the ole' stomach was acting up.

Reencounter with the Barros family

Mário, Laís and MarkBarros, lunch at the port, Salvador

Mário telephoned and we had a fine lunch at a nice restaurant in the old port. "Laís is doing family therapy and has her own office; she spoke of a conference she would be attending for eight days in Fortaleza. Daughter Carla is married to Anderson and they live in Brasília; they met when she was doing a stint of work in Belém do Pará; they are quiet happy as newlyweds.

Son Eduardo has his own band and is currently doing "gigs" in São Paulo.

Mário says his work deals with new techniques for extracting oil in the sea; he as a broker gets Brazilians and foreigners together for joint projects in this area. He travels frequently to Houston and Los Angeles; he looks good, takes care of himself, is very slender but is now balding like yours truly.

We then went to their house in Itapuã and things have changed some: the area is noisier and many people are renting their bungalows to foreigners who come to the beach area for partying and sex. Even the "samba school" Oludum was present one night on the beach and created a racket; the calm and quiet of yesteryear are just a memory.

Mário's mother died and his father lives in Porto Alegre; Mário goes three times a year to Porto Alegre to visit, to check up on things and make sure "Dad" is doing all right. The Barros talk of the scarcity of good medical facilities where they live and are thinking of buying an apartment closer to the city near the doctors. They are thinking of not having to drive as much as they grow older (it seemed a little premature to me, but what do I know; time is passing).

I spoke of our life, of you Keah, and of Katie's film. Mário is totally disillusioned with Brazilian politics (remember this is 2005), including Lula and the MST, of the ever increasing corruption and bureaucracy in Brazil. They still remember the ASU days and old Vanderly the apartment manager where we met and lived in "Sin City" near the university. It was a good encounter; I asked myself in 2005, "Will it be the last?"

Getting about Salvador

On another day there was breakfast at the hotel with a view of the sea, then a comfortable bus to the "Praça da Sé" passing by the old boarding house near Piedade Plaza in the 1960s. The old "Portuguesa" restaurant has gone by the way, sad!

The "Mercado Modelo," Salvador

The historic center looks better, perhaps because the buildings have been painted. I walked to the São Francisco Church, my favorite and the most famous in Bahia and perhaps in all of Brazil: the 17th century Brazilian Baroque with the fat, sensuous angels and the gold gilt interior. I attended a mass which featured a married couple renewing their wedding vows with a choir singing and the harmony of the voices. It was interesting to watch the people at the mass while contemplating the amazing beauty of the church. It was a good time for me, calm and time to meditate and think. The noise of the "Oludum" drums could be heard outside during the mass.

The "Fundação Casa de Jorge Amado" was closed; perhaps I'll go tomorrow. I thought to myself, "I no longer need to worry about such things." The old restaurant I frequented in past times with a view of the bay was also closed.

I walked back to the Lacerda Elevator with its incredible view of the lower city and the bay; there was little traffic and the city was calm. I took the elevator down to the lower city and returned to the "Mercado Modelo," looking good with a new paint job. Rodolfo Coelho Cavalcante's old "cordel" stand was still there on the outside left as you enter the market, but it is closed today (I finally realized today is some kind of a holiday). I went up to the third floor and Camaféu de Oxossi's former bar and restaurant, the place where the "moleque" and his turned on chain saw highlighted the last visit to the place. I did not eat lunch because all they offered was "typical Bahian food" and the ole' stomach was not much interested, so there was a walk back to the Elevator, also remodeled and repainted, in good shape.

I returned to the hotel to my new room on the 23rd floor facing the sea! There was time for a light lunch at the patio pool at 3:30 in the afternoon: a beef filet sandwich, a Coca-Cola and a beer. "I'm writing these notes as I appreciate the view of the ocean at Bahia, enjoying the calm time, writing e-mails home to you, swimming in the pool and to bed at 10:30."

The last day in Bahia was a day of more tourism, really killing time: a relaxing breakfast overlooking the sea, bus to the "Praça da Sé" once again, back to the "Mercado Modelo" and Rodolfo's poetry shop still closed ("I think it is closed permanently, something Carlos Cunha had predicted some years ago.") There was time for a calm visit to the "Igreja de Nossa Conceição da Praia" in the lower city, famous for the procession when the "Baianas" in all their finery carry the statue of the Virgin in pilgrimage to her Son's church in Bonfim ["A Igreja do Nosso Senhor do Bonfim"] where in a "candomblé" ceremony they wash the steps of the outside of the church and then attend mass inside.

Then there ensued a trip up the Elevator again to the "Terreiro de Jesus," the "Pelourinho" and the Jorge Amado Foundation; there was much nostalgia of the old times, my book on Jorge long out of stock and no reprinting. I was fortunate to have a talk with Myriam Fraga, an old friend of days gone by and still director of the Foundation; she seemed surprised and glad to see me. She spoke of the late Jorge ["o saudoso Jorge"] and of Zélia now 89 years old; the latter died after my visit to Brazil in 2005. We spoke of Carlos Cunha and Edilene Matos, she now remarried and with a Ph.D. from the USP. An Aside: One of the girls in the bookstore said my book on Cuíca de Santo Amaro was the most sought after of the entire collection!

There were cultural activities related to the "cordel" everywhere: theater, music and dance; but to the trained, veteran eyes of the old "cordel" researcher there was much "false" stuff, "cordel" as a fad, and nothing of the books of "cordel" in sight. I remembered that I had the first book in Brazil with the title "A Literatura de Cordel." The locals at the FJA suggested I contact Plínio Martins to see if he would be interested in doing the autograph party for "Retrato" in Salvador. Who knows!

I returned to the hotel with the same lunch by the pool ("sanduíce de file, arroz e uma cerveja") and then telephoned Carlos Cunha; "we are supposed to meet tonight at the hotel, but I'm not counting on it."

There has been a lot of time alone in Salvador, a lot of solitude, but I did what I could and it turned out well. I surmise I will be busy enough in João Pessoa and am happy it was left for the end of the trip. There is a "frescão" bus from the airport to the hotel, but the JP folks sent an email saying they would pick me up at the airport. I wrote, "I am sending lots of emails this time from the hotel which is good. I hope you are enjoying the hiking in Colorado. Katie wrote and says she is planning on visiting Courtney. I am experiencing a lot of homesickness and missing you; it will be good to get home and tell you all my stories." Bahia has been a good experience and there are no regrets for coming and spending these few days. (An Aside: This would be the last time until my unexpected part-time job as one of the cultural speakers on Lindblad-National Geographic expeditions and the great trips to Brazil in 2013, 2014 and now 2016.)

From Bahia to João Pessoa and the opening of the conference

By the way the hotel in Bahia was $70 USD a night (the most I ever paid in all the years in Brazil, but knowing it was the last visit, a splurge). After the checkout and a twenty minute wait for the bus, it was clear going to the airport (the bus was 50-60 "reais" less than a taxi).

In the airport I met two well-dressed gentlemen (coat and tie in the heat) who said, "SO YOU ARE THE CURRAN!" "Keah I have told you that they know my work and books in this Brazil, that is, the Brazil of "cordel" and its researchers. Their names were Luís Barreto and Jackson from the research center in Aracajú."

Mark and the ocean at João Pessoa

An employee from the José Américo Foundation picked me up at the airport and after a very long ride we arrived at the modest hotel but with a distant view of the beach of Tambaú – I went to the beach and at least got my feet wet. Later there was room service and a good swim in the hotel pool located on the upper floor with a superb view of the ocean. There was no time for a nap but just a quick shower and a bus to the opening of the conference.

Evidently it was locally a grand social event with some two hundred persons present in almost formal attire. They honored Neuma Fechine Borges, an old friend and research colleague in Brazil for years, even decades – Doctor Honoris Causa from the University of Poitiers. The governor was present as was the Secretary of Culture of the State, Neroaldo a former university professor whom I met at the Recife conference back in 1988. Others were Eduardo Diahty Meneses from Fortaleza, a research colleague, the aforementioned Luís Barreto from the Salvador airport, Ivone Maia from the Rui Barbosa Foundation in Rio de Janeiro (she was responsible for the digitizing of the Leandro Gomes de Barros Collection at the Casa de Rui,) and Rosilene Melo from Paraíba, a young, ambitious and fine scholar of "cordel" in the Northeast.

I found the talks a trifle uninteresting that afternoon (was this because I had been retired from full-time academic work for three years?), but then there was a performance by the singer-poet Oliveira de Panelas, one of the most renowned of the day. His style seemed quite a lot "modernized" compared to my day, but the crowd adored the improvisations.

Researcers Rosilene Melo, Ivone Maia and other friends at the conference

I especially enjoyed meeting and talking to Rosilene Melo, now of the university in Campina Grande; she has a book on the "Lira Nordestina Typography," the present version of the old "Typografia São Francisco" of the old-timer José Bernardo da Silva of my earliest days in Brazil, the "cordel" publishing place in Juazeiro do Norte, Ceará. Funny – I met in 1966 the people she is now researching; she was most curious of my meeting with Zé Bernardo. Yours truly the pioneer once again. Rosilene spoke of the "cordelistas" in Ceará now – the "Malditos," Fanka and added that Abraão Batista of Juazeiro fame had a falling out with the "Lira Nordestina," I do not know why.

Photo Gallery of the "cordel" fair at the conference

"Cordel" poet and woodcut artist Abraão Batista at the "cordel" fair" at the conference

Gerardo and Vânia Frota, the fair at the conference

Marcelo Soares at the fair at the conference

The poet and woodcut artist José Costa Leite at the fair at the conference

Poet Varneci Nascimento at the fair

Encounters at the conference and a long day of talks

I spoke with friend Abraão Batista, with Gerardo Frota from Fortaleza and probably "harvested" some seventy new story-poems (a lot of water under the bridge since serious collecting had stopped around the year 2000 – this was the "new" wave of "cordel" in those years due to writing the story-poem on the computer and printing with the printer to the side.) And I met the young poet originally from Bahia but now living in greater São Paulo, Varneci Nascimento, with whom I had corresponded via email in the recent years.

There was a nice talk with Edilene Matos of those many times in Salvador; she is now remarried to Professor Bruno who was a lawyer in Bahia. Daughter Carole is married and with one child. Edilene now has a Ph.D. from the USP, a new book on Cuíca de Santo Amaro and is working at the famous "Fundos Vila Lobos" of the USP.

Neuma looked older but seemed to me to be doing well (evidently not so well; she died just a short while later after all the years of battling cancer). "There is sadness again because of the loss of old friends and colleagues in Brazil; I feel a bit alone."

That night I just slept so-so and dragged myself out of bed the next morning to catch the José Américo Foundation bus to the conference. There were interesting talks by Ivone of the Casa de Rui Barbosa and by Gerardo on the "cordel" of Abraão Batista.

Then came lunch and we returned at 3:00 p.m. My talk: there were problems with the microphone and they gave me only ten minutes! I said to myself ["falei com os botões"], I traveled 4000 miles for this?"

Singer-poet, researcher and writer José Alves Sobrinho

There were some good moments with the veteran poet, woodcut artist from Condado, Pernambuco, José Costa Leite, important in my book to come, "Retrato." I had a written interview from him in 1967 but had never met him in person. Later there were good talks with Marcelo Soares and José Alves Sobrinho (the co-author with Átila de Almeida of the important "Dictionary of Poets").

I wrote, "Keah you cannot imagine how all these people know about my work, bringing copies of books to sign (the main one "História do Brasil em Cordel" from USP in 1998, 2001), asking for advice on research on "cordel," among them a nephew of Manoel Camilo dos Santos, the former who knows my 1973 book "A Literatura de Cordel," Rosilene Melo from Cajazeiras originally, then Juazeiro, then Campina Grande, other new poets of "cordel" like Varneci Nascimento of São Paulo, and finally, the veteran Abraão Batista of Juazeiro do Norte. I thought: Cantel in 1964, me in 1966!"

Gutenberg Costa, researcher from Rio Grande do Norte and the author at the conference

There was a good talk with Ivone Maia and Fernando from Recife who is working with Roberto Benjamin doing a complete history on the printing process of "cordel," now with better paper and computer and printer to the side. The latter have brought a "renaissance" in the medium which he believes is equal to production in the 1960s. The poets now sell in conferences, in schools and the like, something new and different.

I was exhausted that evening, went to bed at 11:30 and was up the next morning at 6:00 for the trip to Campina Grande to see the Átila de Almeida "cordel" collection now housed at the University of Paraíba in Campina Grande.

There was conversation with José Costa Leite and José Alves Sobrinho who stated that I am, for them, more of a "star" than Raymund Cantel in the old days. All this will pass.

The trip to Campina Grande and the conference

I ended up with a seat in the very back of the bus, across from the incredibly smelly bus bathroom; we had to go the entire way with all the windows open! At the conference Arnaldo Saraiva was given thirty minutes to talk and spoke for an hour; yours truly made a quick commentary, clarifying his use of the term "literatura de cordel." Ha.

I met a professor from India; she used the 1973 book on "cordel" in her thesis. Small world.

Someone bought "História do Brasil em Cordel" in Maputo, Moçambique, and wanted an autograph.

Another tidbit on "cordel:" Antônio Lucena de Mossoró did the woodcut prints for the TV version of "Auto da Compadecida" (recall that Marcelo Soares did the same for the hugely successful "telenovela" "Roque Santeiro").

During lunch I was seated next to Luís Barreto and José Costa Leite.

Professor and researcher Arnaldo Saraiva improvising verse
on the return bus rip from Campina Grande

The return bus ride was extremely entertaining with Arnaldo's improvisation of ribald verse; I had never seen this "human" side to him, but it was difficult to get all the continental Portuguese.

Later there was conversation with Bráulio de Nascimento, Luís Barreto, Ria (famous in Europe for her studies on "cordel,") and Gutemberg da Costa doing fine work on the same in Rio Grande do Norte State. And there were improvisations by a singer-poet who appeared on the Jô Soares national TV show.

All the above and a few more notes below are written in the spirit of just "catching up" on happenings in the many years since my retirement and also really just the opportunity to meet old friends and make many new acquaintances with today's "cordel." The reader may recall that this was indeed my last encounter with the milieu of "cordel."

I learned more of the story of the "poet-reporter" José Soares of old Recife days in the São José Market in the 1960s, this from his son Marcelo (see the notes from my interview below). I would have a wonderful encounter with Marcelo a few years later when he was showing and selling his works in the International Folk Art Market in Santa Fe, New Mexico.

I was invited by Luís Barreto to give a talk in Aracajú, all expenses to be paid, but nothing ever came of it.

There was a short chat with the old-timer Paulo of Mossoró (specializing on banditry in "cordel"); he said my work in the field was "rare" in the good sense.

There are some decisions to be made: do I want to go ahead with these things?

The old "pioneer" planted the seeds and he is now collecting the harvest.

Interview with Marcelo Soares

The last night of the conference, Marcelo Soares, Mark and others from the conference

At the tender age of eight Marcelo began to accompany his father the famous "poet-reporter" José Soares to the fairs and markets of the Northeast interior. Marcelo carried the "folhetos," collected the money from the customers and gave them change while his father "declaimed" the verse. They traveled by bus and even on the backs of burros to the fairs outside of Recife.

José like a good "macho" northeasterner had three separate families (not all that uncommon and seen in various fiction accounts in Literature); Marcelo's half-brother Jerônimo is from the first family, Marcelo from the last. When José died, he left 20,000 "cordel" poems in his poetry stand at Recife and the family in poverty. In all three families there was a total of thirteen children; five survived (ironically the same numbers as Rodolfo Coelho Cavalcante's progeny in Bahia). Marcelo was naturally in a sad state of mind with the death; he would go on to spend ten years in Rio and São Paulo eking out a living. He did woodcuts, the art he learned from José Costa Leite and other artists in the "zona da mata."

In 1992 Marcelo decided to begin writing the story-poems of "cordel" while continuing to do his woodcuts and prints. Things got better; he is married with children and lives in Timbaúba in 2005 (there is much more to his story; since those days he has moved to Recife, has added a career of singing with his own band, and is famous as one of the premier woodcut artists of today's "cordel." It would be in this latter capacity that we met in Santa Fe.) He writes his "cordel" poems in longhand like his father, and then types them on the computer and prints on the computer printer to the side. The woodcut prints for the story-poem covers: he does two copies on a small old press at home, scans into the computer, and then prints the "cordel" cover. He cuts the printed paper, folds it, glues it and the process is complete.

Marcelo is a genuine link to the various generations of "cordel" poets and has a foot in each world, old and modern.

An Aside of Other "Cordel" news: it seems like friend, colleague and research Joseph Luyten suffered a stroke that affected his memory and ability to speak Portuguese. At the end of his life he had returned to speaking the Dutch of his youth (news from Marcelo Soares).

I wrote, "This has been a trip of many ups and downs, but the conference and personal contacts in João Pessoa saved the day." An Aside: My Portuguese had ups and downs as well; it depended on the occasion and the circumstances.

Departure from João Pessoa, a stop in Recife, the arrival in São Paulo and the trip home

The next day marked breakfast in the hotel, packing the bags, a last swim in the hotel pool, an email to Keah, bus to the restaurant, a last short talk with Néuma, bus to the José Américo Foundation, its bus to the airport, all ready for the departure and eventually from São Paulo.

It was a quick twenty minute flight to Recife and then the large TAM airplane to São Paulo, the International Flight I believe. There was an interesting conversation on the plane with a delightful young lady who works for SOFETEL a large hotel chain. She spends two or three days a week traveling to inspect new sites for the hotels and tells me Brazil is set to build "a new Cancún" south of Recife. These are the new times of the new century.

An Aside: The airplanes of my international carrier American Airlines are old and worn; the stewardesses are little attractive compared to the girls on TAM who are the opposite: well dressed in nice uniforms, good makeup, and the male stewards "sharp" in appearance as well. I felt like I was back on Colombia's "Aerocondor" in 1975 except that the Colombians dressed better.

The trip almost turned out badly: there was an hour and forty-five minutes to do the international check in, the lines as long as those at Disneyland in Los Angeles, and the scheduled moment for departure coming ever closer. The passengers were all distraught and angry, especially while waiting in the federal inspection lines. The good news was that all three flights that day actually departed on time; my last flight would pass over the western part of Brazil, Colombia, passing by Cancún and to the west of Miami and Galveston (thus avoiding the bad weather and tropical storms in Florida). The last airline dinner was a pre-dinner drink, salad, beef stroganoff, and good Brazilian bread.

Final thoughts about the trip

These are diverse thoughts on this last academic research trip to Brazil. They will first summarize once again the events of the trip and will be followed by thoughts of the career and the future.

It is no longer a treat to travel internationally by air to Brazil; it is reduced to a "cattle car and no treats," at least if one goes in tourist class.

The hotel in São Paulo was fine and at a fine price; room service food was tasty and not expensive compared to going out. The hotel was in a nice part of São Paulo, the subway a good experience, quick, clean and quiet. The time with Audálio once again and with Vanira was unforgettable; I shall not forget their hospitality (thus a faithful ending to this mini-theme in Brazil for forty years: the unending hospitality shown to me at all social, economic and educational levels).

USP was fine with Plínio and Marilene; I await future developments.

I learned the bus system between airports in São Paulo, economizing a lot from taxi rides; the same with the subway system.

The hotel in Rio was junky in comparison to São Paulo and much overpriced; the restaurant with food by the kilo on a nearby street corner helped compensate for the former.

The beach and sidewalk ["calçada"] at Copacabana were still a pleasure and helped "save the day" for the gringo.

The last visit to the Casa de Rui Barbosa Foundation was all right, but I have little enthusiasm or optimism for contact in the future. The gardens were beautiful as usual and Raquel Valença was gracious in receiving me.

Ex-student and friend Roberto was now a bit mysterious in religious thought and practice, but with the same great personality. He saved the day socially in Rio.

The subway in Rio was fine; one gets away from the pollution, the traffic and the noise.

Overall impression of Copacabana: it was now middle class for sure but the beach was the same, a marvel.

The food was still more reasonable and tasty than in the United States; one could get a meal with wine or beer for around $6 USD. I never went to the "restaurantes de luxo;" I was with the middle class.

Bahia. The room in the hotel, the sea, the food, the pool; they were all fine. I did feel the solitude with the exception of the great reunion with Mário and Laís Barros. Once again I did not get to see Carlos Cunha in spite of the many promises over the telephone for an encounter. But I learned from others that I should not have taken it personally; he treated others the same way. Edilene commented on this in João Pessoa noting he was suffering in those years from real depression.

Tourism was in effect a nostalgia trip: returns to the "Igreja de São Francisco," to the "Pelourinho," to the Jorge Amado Foundation where director Myriam Fraga received me well; to the lower city and the "Mercado Modelo" via the "Elevador Lacerda" and that last visit to the "Igreja de Nossa Senhora da Conceição da Praia." Salvador seemed cleaner and better taken care of. The buses were efficient including the "frescão" to the airport. Yet I thought, "There is no reason to return at least not in the immediate future." I will speak of Lindblad-National Geographic and returns years later in the epilogue.

João Pessoa. In sum it was a good congress, the "intellectualization" of "cordel." There were many good moments with the poets and the "fair" recreated for the conference, people like Abraão Batista, Marcelo Soares, José Costa Leite, José Alves Sobrinho and the new, young generation: Vânia, Gerardo, Varneci, and Francisco Diniz. Their mantra was an old one: "All we want is a place or space to sell our verse." Arnaldo Saraiva was the featured international guest, and he deserved it. Ria was an invited guest from Poitiers. But I think, speaking humbly, that I may have been the guest most sought out for autographs, interviews, advice for theses and maybe to write some prefaces to the same. It was constant, each day.

I got along well with most everyone, "We'll see if Aracajú happens." (It did not.) But it was good to be with Luís Barreto, Jackson, Rosilene Melo, Ivone Maia, Gutenberg Costa, Eduardo Diahty Meneses, and Edilene Matos, longtime friend, host, and research colleague from the years in Salvador. An Aside: Edilene lamented the fact that the vast knowledge of Carlos Cunha was never published, much less not written. As mentioned, he suffered depression after the separation. Son Bruno is now a lawyer. And sadly, Sinésio Alves suffered a debilitating stroke and loss of memory. (He is now deceased.)

The short meeting with José Alves Sobrinho. He was genuinely glad to meet me and had received, I don't know how, a copy of the very positive review I had done on his and Átila's still ground breaking research on "cordel" and the poet-singers (I think it appeared in "Chásqui.")

It was a bit of bad luck with my talk, the limited time, but the Brazilians seemed more upset about it ["chateados"] than I.

The trip to Campina Grande. I immensely enjoyed the bus ride, like "going home" after forty years – ranches with the zebu cattle, the entertaining return with Arnaldo's improvisations, Vânia's jokes, Fátima's husband's jokes, the chance for me to sing "16 tons" and tell the Portuguese astronaut jokes. And it was a hoot to meet the researcher from India.

Other miscellanea: the wonderful night with Marcelo Soares and hearing his story.

Luía Barreto seemed very "smooth," but in the good sense, maybe more like a business man, once again in the good sense, maybe a bit like Mário Barros in Salvador.

Marcus Accioly one of the featured speakers seemed like a bit of a dandy to me and reminded me of Leodevigário de Azevedo Filho in Rio in 1973.

It was difficult for me to feel comfortable with Roberto Benjamin and vice versa I think. I wrote, "He did that seminal article on "folk-communication" and never seemed to leave it. They say he is from a very well-to-do Pernambuco sugar cane family and lives from this, not worrying about the financial situation of "normal" folklorists, teachers and researchers. There was no doubt of his great prestige in those days. A good thing: I found him very understated, knowing when to not talk but just listen. Finally all said he is a great administrator and fund raiser.

The short encounter with José Costa Leite was a bit anti-climactic after all those years, with not great enthusiasm either on his part or mine. Perhaps it was because he still hated the idea of "political" story-poems or poems about politics. He remembered my letters from the 1960s and 1970s; in sum, it was a real pleasure to finally meet the man, a great presence in "cordel."

Rosilene Melo and Maurílio were like the graduate students I never had at ASU, she of Zé Bernardo da Silva fame and he of Manoel Camilo dos Santos.

Most significant was the very brief time with Neuma Fechine Borges and I was delighted to see she finally received her "day in the sun." I said goodbye without knowing it would be the last goodbye.

I wrote, "I don't think there will be another moment like this. Remember the Golden Rule; things turned out well and always will; treat others as you want to be treated. That is what I always did and always will do."

The future seen from 2005

At the least "cordel" will be a good hobby and will help to fill the time in retirement (indeed it did with eight related books published at Trafford and the big one at Ateliê). It was, is and will be my professional vocation.

I thought, "Someone, perhaps a guardian angel (I always think of Riobaldo and Diadorim of "Grande Sertão: Veredas"), I don't know who, was always watching over me. Nothing could have been better than the career I had and enjoyed.

"Keep going, keep breathing and let it flow."

With all my love,

Mark

About The Author

Mark Curran is a retired professor from Arizona State University where he worked from 1968 to 2011. He taught Spanish and Portuguese and their respective cultures. His research specialty was Brazil and its "popular poetry in verse" or the "literatura de cordel" de cordel," and he has published many articles in research reviews and now some sixteen books related to the "cordel" in Brazil, the United States and Spain. Other books done during retirement are of either an autobiographic nature – "The Farm" or "Coming of Age with the Jesuits" - or reflect classes taught at ASU in Luso-Brazilian Civilization, Latin American Civilization or Spanish taught at ASU. The latter are in the series "Stories I Told My Students:" books on Brazil, Colombia, Guatemala, Mexico, Portugal and Spain.

Published Books

A Literatura de Cordel. Brasil. 1973

Jorge Amado e a Literatura de Cordel. Brasil. 1981

A Presença de Rodolfo Coelho Cavalcante na Moderna Literatura de Cordel. Brasil. 1987

La Literatura de Cordel – Antología Bilingüe – Español y Portugués. España. 1990

Cuíca de Santo Amaro Poeta-Repórter da Bahia. Brasil. 1991

História do Brasil em Cordel. Brasil. 1998

Cuíca de Santo Amaro – Controvérsia no Cordel. Brasil. 2000

Brazil's Folk-Popular Poetry – "a Literatura de Cordel" – a Bilingual Anthology in English and Portuguese. USA. 2010

The Farm – Growing Up in Abilene, Kansas, in the 1940s and the 1950s. USA. 2010

Retrato do Brasil em Cordel. Brasil. 2011

Coming of Age with the Jesuits. USA. 2012

Peripécias de um Pesquisador "Gringo" no Brasil nos Anos 1960 ou 'A Cata de Cordel" USA. 2012

Adventures of a 'Gringo' Researcher in Brazil in the 1960s. USA. 2012

A Trip to Colombia – Highlights of Its Spanish Colonial Heritage. USA. 2013

Travel, Research and Teaching in Guatemala and Mexico – In Quest of the Pre-Columbian Heritage

Volume I – Guatemala. 2013

Volume II – Mexico. USA. 2013

A Portrait of Brazil in the Twentieth Century – The Universe of the "Literatura de Cordel." USA. 2013

Fifty Years of Research on Brazil – A Photographic Journey. USA. 2013

Relembrando - A Velha Literatura de Cordel e a Voz dos Poetas. USA. 2014

Aconteceu no Brasil – Crônicas de um Pesquisador Norte Americano no Brasil II, USA. 2015

It Happened in Brazil – Chronicles of a North American Researcher in Brazil II. USA, 2015

Diário de um Pesquisador Norte-Americano no Brasil III. USA, 2016

Diary of a North American Researcher in Brazil III. USA, 2016

Professor Curran lives in Mesa, Arizona, and spends part of of the year in Colorado. He is married to Keah Runshang Curran and they have one daughter Kathleen who lives in Albuquerque, New Mexico. Her documentary film "Greening the Revolution" was presented most recently in the Sonoma Film Festival in California. Katie was named best female director in the Oaxaca Film Festival in Mexico.

The author's e-mail address is: profmark@asu.edu

His website address is: www.currancordelconnection.com